Stories by
Carlo Rossi

Edited and Forward by
Tim Williamson

10,000 Dogs (and other assorted creatures)
My 32 Years with the Windsor/Essex County
Humane Society

Copyright © 2019 Carlo Rossi and Tim Williamson

All rights reserved. No part of this book may be used or reproduced in any manner whatsoever, including graphic, electronic or mechanical, including photocopying, recording, taping or by any information storage retrieval system, without written permission of the authors, except in the case of brief quotations embodied in critical articles or reviews. For information, contact Rossi-Williamson, 8445 Riverside Drive E., Windsor, Ontario, Canada N8S 1G1,

10thousanddogs@gmail.com

ISBN: 978-1-9990148-2-7
ISBN: 978-1-9990148-1-0
ISBN: 978-1-9990148-0-3

Published by Amazon Publishing

THIS BOOK IS NOT AUTHORIZED NOR HAS IT BEEN APPROVED IN ANY WAY BY EITHER THE O.S.P.C.A. OR THE WINDSOR/ESSEX COUNTY HUMANE SOCIETY.

PRIOR TO PUBLICATION, THE HUMANE SOCIETY WAS NOT CONSULTED, NOR WERE ANY OF ITS EMPLOYEES, PAST OR PRESENT.

ALL STORIES COME FROM THE MEMORY OF CARLO ROSSI.

THE BOOK IS NOT INTENDED IN ANY WAY AS A CRITIQUE OR EXPOSE OF THE GREAT PEOPLE – EMPLOYEES, MANAGEMENT, DIRECTORS - OF THE WINDSOR/ESSEX COUNTY HUMANE SOCIETY, ONE OF WINDOR'S FINEST INSTITUTIONS.

ADOPT A STRAY, SPAY OR NEUTER YOUR PETS.

Foreword by Tim Williamson

In 2015, the year Carlo Rossi was last at the Windsor/Essex County Humane Society, the place wasn't much different from the shelters at other Canadian Humane Societies. Animal shelters are the focal point of a whole lot of human and animal activity, and Windsor was no exception.

The facility at the time was open to the public seven days a week, between the hours of 9am to 6pm, with some staff on 24 hour call. About 25 people worked there at any given time. The building consisted of administration offices, the manager's office, the intake office, the pound area, and the adoption area. A full-time veterinarian and two AHTs (Animal Health Technicians), had their own office and clinic. In 2011, a public spay-neuter clinic was opened in the Windsor facility.

Entering the one-story building brought you immediately to the intake office, an area which consisted of desks, phones, computers, and five filing cabinets - a typical public office. It was here people brought in strays they'd found, Rossi and his co-workers brought in sick or injured animals for treatment, family pets came to be euthanized, people walked in with complaints and inquiries. It was at times a very busy and emotional place.

There were three women on staff when Carlo was there. Denise, Lori, and the late Jeanne. Jeanne and Denise were responsible for animal intake. Lori handled adoptions. They all shared the telephones and dispatch duties. Rossi worked in the back area of the building, known as the pound area, where all the intake dogs and cats and wildlife were housed. His primary function, in addition to dispatch and rescue, was to take in and care for all these animals. The pound area was divided into 19 indoor runs, 6 indoor/outdoor runs. These areas were primarily for the larger dogs. The smaller dogs were kept in cages in an area known simply as the dog room. He literally saw over 10,000 dogs during the 32 years he was there.

There were two rooms for the cats, each holding approximately 30 cats, all in separate cages. Their cages were stainless steel and contained food water and a litter pan, the cage lined with newspaper. Sick or quarantined cats were kept in a separate room.

Carlo was responsible for feeding and caring for the animals, keeping their areas clean, maintaining order (sometimes not so easy). It was almost never quiet. Hearing protection was not advisable as he had to be much aware of the surroundings. A dangerous dog may get loose. A cat could get its paw caught in a part of the cage and howl to high heaven. There were occasional unwanted animal interactions, fights that had to be broken up.

He was an unsung hero in many ways, big and small – from the wretched horror of removing 320 dogs that had to be euthanized, to rescuing a squirrel caught in a chain link fence, or removing a fishing line tangled around a Canada Goose's leg. He took pride in wearing the Humane Society uniform, and wouldn't change a thing if he had a chance.

He saved countless dogs, cats and other creatures in different predicaments, was saddened when he couldn't, and encountered a wide, maddening and amusing array of animals and humans.

What follows is a sometimes irreverent, sometimes sad, sometimes happy, sometimes humorous, sometimes surprising, sometimes shocking, but always passionate account taken from over three decades of front line animal rescue experiences, as told by my friend of 50 years, Carlo Rossi.

Tim Williamson
Windsor, Canada
May 04, 2019

TABLE OF CONTENTS

Chapter 1 – page 1

NIGHT PATROL - *o solo mio* danger- angry people sometimes – a dog dangerously dangling off a balcony

Chapter 2 – page 7

STRAY DOGS – stuck in the middle of the alley with you – airport dog control – officer fires warning shot at loose rottweiller - free ride from transit windsor – expressway close call

Chapter 3 – page 21

A HORSE IS A HORSE OF COURSE – runaway chestnut on riverside drive – zee great italian equine detective

Chapter 4 – page 29

DEER FRIENDS AND OTHER CREATURES – habitat threat to the deer – american deer crosses the detroit river to check downtown windsor's wonders

Chapter 5 – page 53

EARS TO YOU MISTER – terrible animal abuse story from windsor with a happy ending

Chapter 6 – page 59

PUPPY MILLS – humane society removes 320 dogs from out-of-control breeder in the county

Chapter 7 – page 65

TATTOO YOU – biker turns tables on dog abuser

Chapter 8 – page 71

CATS – who would have thought I had acrophobia – kitten goes down the drain – limit of 2 cats per household gets exceeded by nutty cat lovers - so that's how the traps work

Chapter 9 – page 85

DON'T TRY THIS AT HOME – dog removed from downtown house

Chapter 10 – page 89

EMERGENCY WORK – traffic and canines don't mix well – three dogs struck by same vehicle

Chapter 11 – page 95

LOYALTY OF DOGS – faithful dogs get dropped off for good – return to the animal abusers scene of the crime

Chapter 12 – page 101

DOGS IN MY HEAD – my two dog basic rules – the barking never stops – guard dogs with bad attitudes – wonton soup on the house

Chapter 13 – page 105

DANGEROUS KILLER DOGS – pit bull dogs seized from dog fighting ring – albino american pit bull terrier trained to go for the throat

Chapter 14 – page 109

DOGS, DOGS, AND MORE DOGS – basic rules – buddy the chow

Chapter 15 – page 115

POLICEMEN ARE YOUR FRIENDS – working well with the men and women in blue – people die, where their pets go

Chapter 16 – page 123

CIRCUS INSPECTIONS – protests – all kinds of animals to check on – angus the famous elephant

Chapter 17 – page 129

LIFE AT THE SHELTER – it's a family affair – fritz did it – shelter stand-off – windsor loves cats and dogs and proves it – yuletide shelter celebrations

Chapter 18 – page 139

MASCOTS – humane society gets pick of the litter – such characters – a famous windsor downtown dog

Chapter 19 – page 153

SHORT NOTES – mr. hockey – liberated hound - high school kids at the shelter

ADDENDUM – page 164
criminal code sections, ospca act sections – windsor city by-law

BIOS – page 172

10,000 DOGS (and other assorted creatures)

My 32 years with the Windsor/Essex County Humane Society

"The greatness of a nation and its moral progress can be judged by the way its animals are treated"

Mohandas Gandhi

Putting Windsor on the map

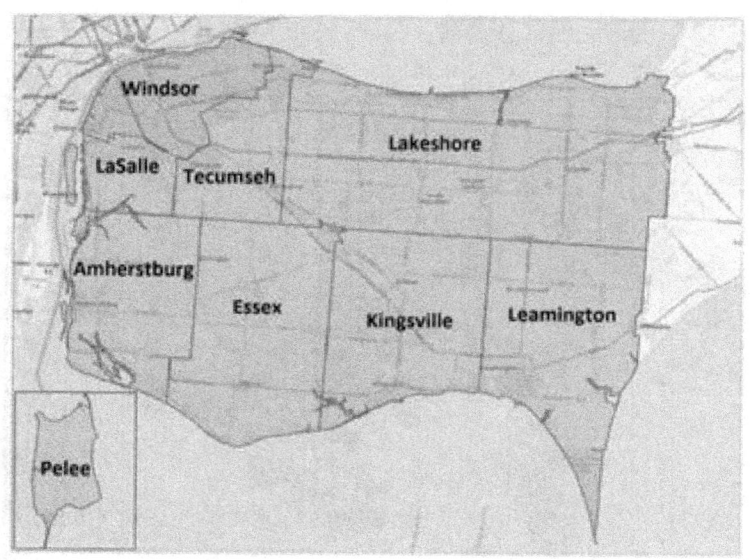

Essex County – Windsor/Essex County Humane Society Jurisdiction

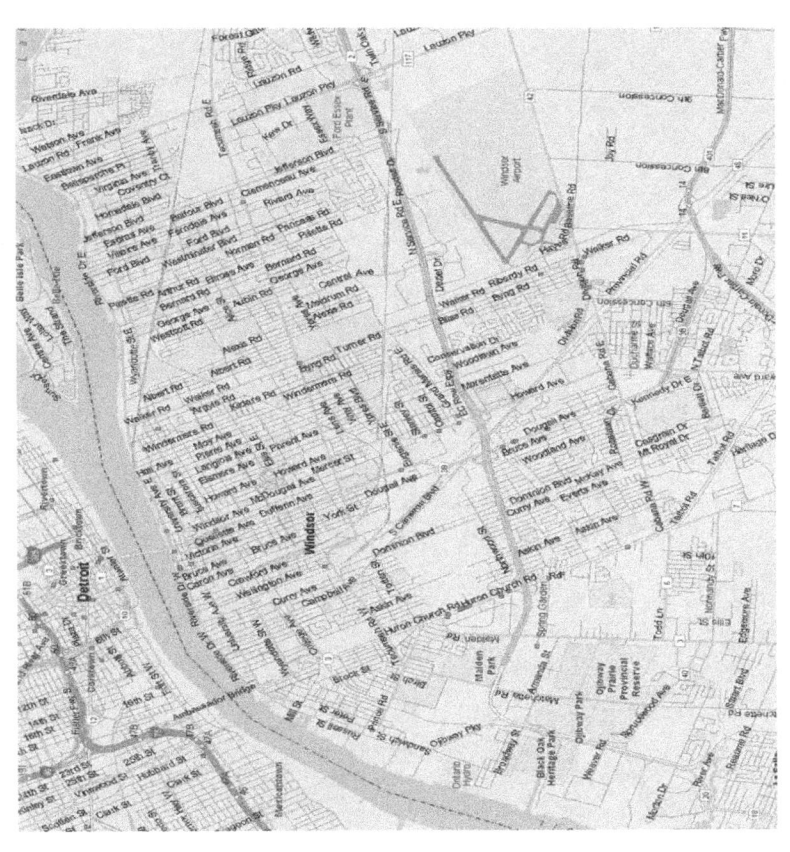

Street Map – City of Windsor

CHAPTER ONE – night patrol – a murder suspect, a balcony, and a very big problem

Working the 4pm to midnight shift for almost 5 years was a solitary endeavour. With few exceptions, I worked alone, and sometimes in dangerous situations.

thinking ahead

One night I received a call to pick up a *confined stray*, humane society lingo for a stray dog held by someone other than the owner. When I got to the address, a woman had a spaniel mix type dog in her front porch. I asked the lady if she knew where the dog lived. She said she did not. I brought the dog to my van and was in the process of securing it when a large man came from out of nowhere, and slammed me down to the ground with such a force that I was knocked out of my shoes. He then stood over me with his fists moving around and angrily said *"Get up!"* I got up as he said, but quickly proceeded, without my shoes, to the radio and called our office requesting immediate police assistance. Thankfully, the Humane Society had a great working relationship with the various police departments in Windsor and Essex County. I anxiously awaited their arrival (being a teenager during the 1960s, ironic, me looking forward to the police). Meanwhile the man, who turned out to be the dog's owner, was concentrating his attention on the lady who called us, and had her down on the ground choking her. The police quickly arrived and within seconds tackled, handcuffed, arrested, and took the guy away.

Apparently, he lived right next door to the lady who had called us. The police told me that the man had a criminal record and had just gotten out of jail the week before. The police charged the man for the assault on the lady. They, along with my boss, wanted me to press charges for me getting assaulted as well. I declined, stating, *"I'm working alone every night, you know how it is, right Officer?"* I figured this guy was going to get out of jail eventually, and I just wanted things to end there and then.

like whatever, dude

Another night I received a call about a dog owner who I was told repeatedly let his dog run loose in the neighbourhood. I arrived at the address on Caron Avenue, a street known to the authorities. It was an unkempt house in the inner core of the downtown area. A man in his twenties answered the door. I identified myself and told him it was against the city by-law to have his dog constantly running at large on city streets. He argued with every point I was making. Finally I told him, *"Look buddy, you can't be a rebel all your life. Just take care of your dog."* He gave me a dismissive *"Whatever"*, and slammed the door. The dog was home at the time so I just left thinking I would probably be back there again at some time for the same problem, and give him a ticket then. I never had to go back, because two weeks later I found out that he was in jail, held without bail on a murder charge for which he was ultimately convicted and sentenced to twenty-five years. I wonder how that rebel thing is working out for him now.

ye shall hang by the neck

At the beginning of my shift one day in 1986, I was dispatched on a call about a dog in distress at an address on Crawford Avenue. The caller stated there was *"a dog hanging by the neck over a balcony railing"*.

I got there as fast as I could. Sure enough, I saw an adult shepherd mix black and tan, hanging by its collar over the second story balcony railing of a two-story walk-up apartment building. The dog was struggling mightily, but quietly, as it was actually choking and couldn't bark or squeal. I had to act fast. With no one home where the dog was, I quickly got a ladder from the neighbour who had made the call, he himself freaking out at this poor dog choking to death.

I climbed the ladder, got on the balcony and was about to use the railing to support myself when I realized the railing was not anchored very well to the floor of the balcony. This made the job way more difficult, because the dog weighed about 65 lbs. I then proceeded to pull the scared dog towards me, pulled it up and placed it on the balcony floor, when it tried to bite me. This was one frightened and p*#sed off canine.

By this time the owner of the dog had come home, saw me and the dog on his balcony, and quickly ran up the stairs and into his apartment. He opened the sliding door, and I brought the dog in. I checked the dog over and it actually appeared OK. I warned the owner not to leave the dog on the balcony again.

He looked at me and said, *"No sh*t".*

CHAPTER TWO – stray dogs – airport dog - who let these dogs out – stuck in the middle with you

If I didn't have any calls to take care of on the night shift, I was supposed to drive around in the Humane Society van and look for any trouble. I had to patrol all "the projects", and a few other areas where we received the most complaints about dogs running at large. The city by-law prohibited owners from allowing their dogs to run loose. Cats were and still are exempt both from licence requirements and running loose rules. Kitties have been off the hook for this for centuries.

> **WINDSOR/ESSEX COUNTY HUMANE SOCIETY**
>
> **DOGS RUNNING AT LARGE**
>
> No dog shall run at large in any street, lane, alley, park or in any other public place in the municipality, but shall be kept securely chained or confined on the premises of the owner, and if found running at large shall be seized and taken to the Windsor/Essex County Humane Society, 1375 Provincial Road by our Animal Control Officer.
>
> The owner of any dog impounded at the Humane Society may redeem the same within seventy-two hours by paying a fee. If the dog is not redeemed it may be sold or destroyed.
>
> In addition to the impounding and destruction provided for, the owner of any dog running at large may be liable to a penalty for each offence of not more than $50.00, exclusive of costs, and such penalty and costs shall be recoverable under the provisions of the Summary Convictions Act.

Consider this a warning
(Photo S. Vesala)

You can't outrun a dog, but you can definitely follow a stray with your vehicle down streets and alleys, and even do it driving backwards, if necessary. My night vision was very good, better than most people. I could spot a dog from two blocks away. My approach was to follow the dog as closely as possible and then try to catch it. If I couldn't, I would follow the dog, sometimes across busy streets, and if I was lucky, follow it to its home. If a dog had crossed any busy streets, I would usually issue a ticket, but sometimes I just gave a warning. If the dog was almost hit by a car, I would always gladly give out a ticket.

When I was able to tag a loose dog, and found out where it lived (usually just by calling in the dog licence number), I would go to the address and knock on the door. The person would answer, and I would ask if he or she owned a dog, and where it was. Sometimes they would go to the back yard and look for the dog, or just say they didn't know. I would then tell the owner that the dog was in my van, and that I would have to issue a ticket for the dog running at large.

```
Pound Record Card
                                              No 40856
Date in _____
                        Time                  On Arrival
                             a.m.
Owned ☐   Truck _____ pm                    Sick    ☐
                             a.m.
Stray  ☐  Pound _____ pm                    Injured ☐
                                              Dead    ☐
Location _____
Breed of Animal _____
Dog   ☐              M ☐              Spayed    ☐
Cat   ☐              F ☐              Neutered  ☐
Other ☐                               Declawed  ☐
Windsor License # _____  Misc. # _____
                       Description
Est. Age _____       Est. Weight _____
                          Mark or
Colour _____        Collar _____
Owner: _____ Phone: _____
Address: _____

Sold ☐       Claimed ☐            Destroyed ☐
Other ☐ _____

Pound Keeper's Signature _____ Date Out _____
Feed:   Dry   Canned   Puppy Chow   Kitten Chow
Vaccines Given: _____
Treatments Given: _____
_____
Veterinarian's Comments: _____
_____
General Comments: _____
_____
```

This could be your dog
(Photo S. Vesala)

Some people would get smooth with me and say *"Keep the dog then"*, to which I would reply *"You're going to get the ticket anyway so you may as well take your dog. But don't be angry. It's not the animal's fault"*. What they didn't realize was that I was saving them money, because if the dog went to the pound, it was going to cost twice as much as the ticket to get the dog back. And some of these people were scary.

Neighborhood kids usually knew where all the dogs lived. If I was following a loose dog across streets and saw some kids playing nearby, I would ask them if they knew where the dog lived. They would almost invariably tell me which house it was. With gratitude, I would return to the kid who told me the correct location and give the little informer a buck. In certain parts of the city, I had built up a network of smart street kids, willing to give me vital information.

There was an older boy, about 18 or so, who lived in one of the poorest areas of Windsor at the time, the downtown core, just east of the casino. He knew everybody in the neighbourhood, and helped me locate owners more than once. Sometimes I gave him cigarettes instead of money. He had been born into poverty and never really had a chance. He died in his twenties. I digress.

doggy heat, not the movie - stuck in the alley with you

When female dogs were in season, please pardon the expression, activities ramped up. Dogs will be dogs, after all.

Driving in the van one sunny spring afternoon, I received a call from dispatch about two dogs *"intertwined and running loose"*. I arrived at the scene, which was on Drouillard Rd., in the former Ford City. I saw both dogs, but they quickly ran into an alley, where I caught up with them. They were very much stuck to each other, okay, but the female was facing one way and the male was facing in the opposite direction, something I had never seen before. It looked painful for both dogs, so I figured I didn't want to start chasing them and risk making it worse. Halfway down the alley, they suddenly disappeared into a backyard. I got out of the truck and ran towards the yard, which luckily had a gate. I stepped into the yard and closed the gate behind me, a method I had used many times when capturing stray dogs. Luckily the front gate was also closed. The dogs were now confined. The male was a terrier, the female a spaniel mix. I put a leash on the female and then I turned the terrier around to the normal breeding position. Then I just waited, keeping both dogs calm. Eventually the male became free from the female, and they decoupled. Having both dogs separated and leashed, I knocked on the back door of the house where I was and asked the gentleman who came to the door if he owned either of the two dogs. He said no, so I returned to the shelter with the two dogs. We looked both of them over. They appeared OK. I left a note on their ID cards for the veterinarian to check them both out in the morning, which she did. All was well. Nobody came to claim either of these dogs, so they were adopted out separately, both happy and healthy. With gleams in their eyes.

air traffic dog control

Stray dogs on city streets can be dangerous to traffic and themselves. Just as dangerous, maybe more so but in a different way, is a loose dog on an airport property.

We got a call on a Saturday afternoon about a stray dog running loose at the Windsor Airport. Because of the wide open area we expected to have to cover, I took my partner Norm with me. The airport had told us we needed to work as quickly as possible because of the danger to any plane (and passengers) landing or taking off. We soon saw the dog, a brown spaniel/collie type dog, right in the middle of the expansive airport property. We tried to coax the dog over to us, with no luck. We split up, Norm in the truck, and me on foot. Again, no luck. We were going in circles.

I finally saw our little friend near the runway approach. I got about 30 feet away from the very confused dog when it started running away again. I yelled "STOP" at the top of my voice. The dog stopped in its tracks for a few seconds and I quickly put the leash on it, and got it off the airport property. Mission accomplished.

dogs like rules

I had done the exact same thing a few weeks before at the kennels when a volunteer was walking by some portable metal cages on her way out to walk a small terrier type. The woman had the dog on a leash. Suddenly, a mean pit bull busted out of its cage and headed straight for the terrier. I yelled *"STOP"* at the top of my lungs, and the pit bull actually stopped moving, allowing me to quickly put the leash on it and return it to its kennel. A narrow escape for the little terrier. The pit bull would have either severely injured or killed the smaller dog. And possibly injured the volunteer, or worse.

not a clean shot

In 1994, we received a call one afternoon from Windsor Police about a large dog running loose in a posh neighbourhood just west of the Southwood Lakes area. The police were already there when I arrived. I knew both cops. One of them, let's call him *Fearless Fosdick*, I knew liked dogs. I saw the large rottweiler, black and brown, which I estimated at a good 100 lbs. My first attempt to catch the dog was unsuccessful. I followed the dog a little further, but it abruptly turned around and started heading straight for me. I stretched my leash out, but the dog went right by me. It then started heading towards one of the two police officers who were 20 feet behind me. When the dog wouldn't stop, *Fosdick* drew his Smith & Wesson and fired it to the side of the dog to scare it, but the bullet accidentally grazed the dog's right ear. The gunshot scared me, I have to say. The dog then veered away and I proceeded to chase it. I don't know how I did it, but I caught up to the dog and put my leash on it. The dog seemed frightened, and I noticed his right ear had some blood on it. I took the dog to Walker Road Emergency Animal Clinic so the dog could be examined by a veterinarian.

(Photo from dicktracy.info)

Getting shot by the Windsor police turned out to be only a minor injury for the dog. While I was at the clinic, a biker type person dressed in black leather arrived, stating he was the owner of the rottweiller. I explained the dog was running loose and ran towards a police officer who fired a warning shot to the side of the dog to scare it away. He didn't seem too happy to hear this, but I pointed out that it could have been a lot worse. The guy abruptly left with his dog in tow, less part of its bandaged ear. And he didn't even say thank you, or anything.

code blue, whoopee, a free bus ride from a friendly transit driver - one lucky dog

The Humane Society Shelter is located on a very busy street, on Provincial Road in South Windsor at Cabana Road. Any dog escaping the building was a potentially dangerous occurrence. Whenever that happened, there was a notification over the intercom that there was a *Code Blue*. We always knew something was up when we heard this.

On one Code Blue, a large German shepherd managed to escape the facility. Seeing it happen, I ran after the dog, which was running south on Provincial Road. The traffic was busy. I ran until I was out of breath, struggling to keep up with the liberated canine. I continued as best I could, with the dog way ahead of me. Suddenly, a passing city bus stopped next to me. The door opened to a bus packed with people. The bus driver yelled "*Get in*", he having witnessed my struggle from his panoramic vantage point. I got on the bus and we easily caught up to the shepherd. By this time we had almost reached Walker Road, a fair distance. I saw the dog near a business, thanked the bus driver for the ride, got off the bus and proceeded toward the dog. Luckily I was able to get the dog on the leash I was carrying. It was going to be a long way back to the shelter. Fate again on my side,

Carol, (favourite volunteer) had noticed which way I had gone, showed up with her SUV, and picked up me and the dog-escapee.

Hiram Walker, from the archives of
Hiram Walker and Sons

Walker Road is a major artery in Windsor, named after one of the city's most famous citizens, Hiram Walker. (1816-1899) Walker moved to Detroit from Massachusetts at age 22. He dabbled in various businesses, one of them distilling vinegar in barrels, followed by whisky, which he distilled in what is now Windsor, at Hiram Walker & Company, selling lots of it during the Civil War. He built a ferry system across the Detroit River, a railway to southern Essex County, roads, public buildings, mills, distilleries and churches in the Windsor area. He was the first mayor of the village of Walkerville, where he personally funded street construction, lighting, firefighters and police services. At one time he owned 10,000 acres along the river in Windsor and Sandwich. He had a casino on Lake Erie. Walker willed all his real estate to Detroit area hospitals. The distillery, sold in 1936, is still in operation. (distilled from Wikipedia)

lucky lab

Late one summer night in 1998, I was headed home in my own car on E.C Row Expressway when I noticed a black Labrador retriever running loose. This dog was in big-time danger. I stopped and got out of my car with a bungee cord because I didn't have a leash with me. The dog noticed me and ran towards the median. I carefully followed. Now on the grassy area between the Howard and Dougall overpasses, I figured the dog would be OK as long as he stayed in the median. I got closer just as it was nearing the overpass. The lab looked scared as it got closer to the small metal guardrail it now faced. Beyond the guardrail was a 30 ft. drop to the pavement of Dougall Avenue. I proceeded slowly, trying to reassure the dog that everything was OK. I got close enough to put the bungee around the dog's neck. This could have been a life and death situation for the dog. I brought the dog back to my car, a fair distance away. By now it was 1:30 am. Since I had to go in to work the next morning, I went home thinking I would put the dog in my garage until morning. Just as I was opening the back door of the garage, the bungee cord broke and the dog ran away and was soon out of sight.

I was upset about the bungee breaking and me losing the lab, but at least it didn't get injured on the Expressway. I went to work the next morning and started my regular work day. One hour later, someone called the shelter stating there was a Labrador retriever barking in their back yard. It was my friend from the Expressway.

We went and picked it up, big smiles on our faces, dog included.

CHAPTER THREE – a horse is a horse of course - I wanna tell my tail, c'mon – you're a horse's tail

We inspected the stables every year at the old Windsor Raceway, where for years they held harness races you could bet on. I did inspect the stables. And occasionally bet. With some degree of success.

Actually, I'm afraid of horses. You can't control a horse like you can control a dog with a leash or a catchpole. They are big, really big. Too big. You never know what a horse will do unannounced, like kick you in the shins, give you a head butt, charge at you, rear up on you, bite you, or any combination thereof.

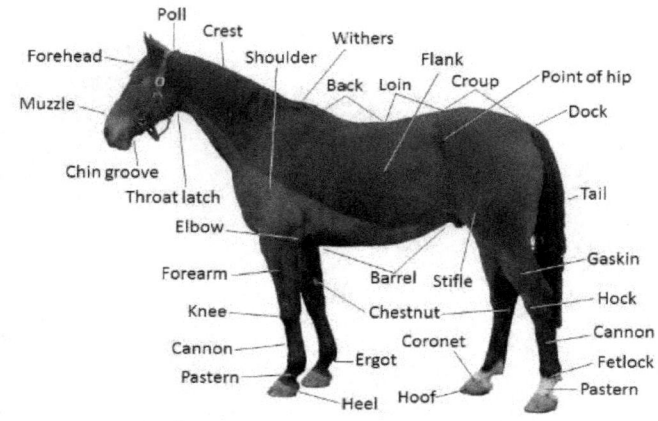

(Photo Wikimedia.org/wikipedia)
Fun horse fact: a hand = four inches

silver and kemo sabe

On one hot and humid Windsor summer night in July of 1987, I received a call on my pager around 3 am about a runaway horse seen on Riverside Drive, across from Sand Point Beach on Lake St. Clair, in the Riverside area of the city. Thinking it was a hoax (they happened), I checked in with the answering service. They gave me the phone number of the caller, and I quickly verified that it was a real call about a real horse on the loose. Great.

I found the field, and sure enough, in the middle was a young (3 or 4 year old) chestnut coloured horse. I had already contacted the police. With much trepidation, I walked over and grabbed the bridle of the now very nervous and jumpy horse. I was more afraid than I would have been walking into a room with 5 pit bulls. I just kept saying "*WHOA*", like *The Lone Ranger*, praying the horse would stay put.

(Photo post-gazette.com)

The Lone Ranger was a popular American television series which ran from 1949 to 1957. It started in the 1930s as a low budget serial on radio station WXYZ in neighbouring Detroit (people in Windsor have always listened to Detroit radio stations, though not exclusively). Gioachino Rossini's iconic *William Tell Overture* was chosen as the theme song, in large part due to it being in public domain and therefore free to use. Initially expected to be a flop, the Lone Ranger radio serial was so quickly successful it was picked up by a national network, and ran 2,956 weekly episodes 1933-

1954. The Lone Ranger's horse was *Silver*. Robin Seymour, Windsor radio station giant CKLW "The Big 8"' DJ star and host of the Windsor/Detroit TV show *Swingin' Time*, was a child actor on the radio show. Jay Silverheels (Harold Jay Smith), played Tonto on the television series. He was a Canadian Six Nations Mohawk from Brantford, Ontario. Silverheels (Smith), was a superb lacrosse player, boxed professionally, raised horses, acted and was a stuntman in dozens of movies, including parts in *Key Largo* and *True Grit*. His horse in the TV series was called *Scout*.

There was a municipal grandfathered zone south of Riverside Drive where horses were still allowed to be stabled amidst the new large homes that were going up at a rapid pace, and I guessed, correctly, this chestnut had just busted loose from a stable there.

The next half an hour seemed like an eternity, me worried, holding on to a big, excited and jumpy young horse by the bridle, all by myself, at 3:30 in the morning. The police had contacted a man through the then up and running Windsor Raceway who had a horse trailer. He arrived soon enough, and he gently led the horse into the trailer. This involves pulling the horse up a ramp and squeezing alongside it to the front of the trailer, then hitching the bridle line to the post at the front of the trailer. The average horse weighs between 380 and 1,000 *kilograms*, so imagine one stepping on your foot.

The horse safely in the trailer, I breathed a sigh of relief. The next morning, the fellow who owned the horse called the Humane Society about a lost horse. He contacted the guy with the trailer, and he soon went and picked up his horse.

carlo rossi, horse detective

In the fall of 1983 we received a complaint about two horses that were not being adequately cared for, apparently abandoned. This is against the law, and everybody knows it.

I arrived at the location, which was a couple of miles south of Windsor on County Rd 9, almost at County Rd 8, which dissects Essex County. I spoke to the elderly man who called us and learned that he owned the stables and rented them out to individual horse owners. He stated that the two horses he was worried about belonged to a couple of brothers who were renting their stables from him, and that he hadn't seen very of much of them lately. The barn had about 10 stalls for horses. I went inside the building where he showed me the two horses, a bay mare and its foal, a young brown colt. There was a small amount of food (hay and oats), and water was available. The stall was relatively clean. The mare appeared a little thin to me, but the colt appeared OK. The stable owner told me the names of the two brothers, but didn't have an address for them. He did know they frequented Windsor Raceway, and after making inquiries at the Raceway, I went to an address tip I got from someone in the stables, only to learn they didn't live there anymore. I wanted to warn them they could be charged with animal neglect. I actually wanted to charge them. The Humane Society took these things very seriously. So did I.

Two days later I returned to the stable and found only water for the horses, who had now finished their oats and hay. I drove to the local Co-Op, picked up some feed, and brought it to the now very hungry horses. Again, the mare seemed a little thin, the foal not so much. The kindly stable owner, who appeared to be in his eighties, told me he would provide the horse with straw and water, and clean the stalls.

I checked out nearby stables asking about these two brothers, with no luck. I checked out the stables belonging to Windsor Raceway and talked to regulars, horse trainers and owners. Racetracks are their own communities – everybody knows each other and what they're up to. Racetracks are a lot like little unincorporated villages.

And it was there that I got my first good lead. A guy I spoke to knew the two brothers and told me that they didn't own the horses, but were only leasing them. After further investigation I found out the name of the actual owner of the mare and its foal. The Humane Society then contacted the man who was the owner. He lived in the Kent Bridge area just east of Chatham, Ontario, outside of our jurisdiction. Two days later we met him at the stables. A local veterinarian looked over the two horses. He said the foal was in better shape than the mare, but no steps needed to be taken. With the horses loaded into the trailer, we knew they were on their way to a better life. We never did find the two idiot brothers to hold them accountable. I wanted to, trust me.

A year later, the owner came to the shelter and told us that the mare had died, but the colt was a strong and healthy "*Fireball*".

CHAPTER FOUR – deer friends and other wildlife - can't matchette rd. - opossums, raccoons and skunks oh my - sorry, wainwright and prine – a dining delicacy

A lot of deer live in the Windsor-Essex county area. Many of these deer live within the boundaries of the City of Windsor proper, and most of these live in the southwest part of the city. It seemed to me that the Windsor deer were more people friendly than their cousins in the county.

The Windsor deer were getting cornered. I'm referring to the South Cameron Woodlot, between

Totten Rd. and the Expressway, Dominion and Huron Church Rd, an area of about 5 square miles. Houses were going up at a fast pace (still are). A large school replaced a natural orchard, further encroaching on habitat. A lot of deer used to live there, but not so much anymore. They call it progress.

poor deer

I received a call one night about a deer that had been hit by a car on Matchette Road. I arrived just around 10:30pm. The road was jam-packed with traffic from Windsor Raceway. The 150 lb white-tailed adult was in the ditch on the east side of the road, still alive, both its front legs broken. It was frantically trying to get out of the ditch, but even if it could, with all the traffic going by, it would easily get struck by another car.

I got a rope from my van. The deer was next to a telephone pole so I managed to tie the rope around the deer and the pole at the same time. When I was sure the deer could not move, I went back to my van and called for the veterinarian on call who showed up in under 20 minutes. He quickly assessed the situation. With two broken legs, there was only one option. The deer had to be euthanized to prevent more suffering.

ray, a tranquilizer gun - man has entered the tool and die factory work yard with a tranquilizer rifle

When I first started at the Humane Society, we had our own tranquilizer gun, which was kept safely under lock and key. The necessary anaesthetics were also locked up, but separately. We loaded and deployed the gun ourselves (with the vet's general permission). Later, we needed the vet to provide and load the dart with the drugs in it into the gun, before we used it. While I was at the Humane Society, I only saw the tranquilizer gun used 10 times. By the time I left in 2015, we stopped using tranquilizer guns altogether. Then, it was the police that had to shoot injured deer if we couldn't get them back to safety in their habitat.

tunnel vision

On a fall day in 1983, the Humane Society received a call about a deer running around in downtown Windsor. We located it, and chased it into one of many active factory yards in Windsor. Somebody called 9-1-1. Our plan was to corner the deer so we could tranquilize it. This took some tactical talent. Six or seven of us, cops included, converged on the deer, but it was having none of it, and ran right at us, jumping right over the head of one of the police officers. We eventually cornered it again, and the deer was quickly tranquilized.

The deer now down, the veterinarian said it wasn't a Canadian white-tailed, but, he figured, a deer that came to Windsor by swimming across the Detroit River, across the Canada/USA boundary, which goes down the middle of the river, probably from Belle Isle, a stone's throw from the Canadian side. Belle Isle is lovely municipal park on an island owned by the City of Detroit. Turns out it was indeed a European fallow deer, likely a descendant from the herd of them originally given by the President of France to the soon-to-be called Motor City in 1895. These 2 different types of deer, the white-tailed, and the European fallow, can't mix or breed.

European Fallow Deer
(123rf.org)

White-tailed Deer
(en.wikipedia.org)

We placed the unconscious deer in the Humane Society van, tied its four legs with rope, and secured the animal for transport. The office called the park manager on Belle Isle in Detroit to alert them that a border-jumping deer was headed back to its American home.

We proceeded to the Windsor/Detroit Tunnel, which ordinarily would have been the fastest way to Belle Isle. We were waived through without paying the tunnel fare. Unfortunately for us, it was the busiest time of the day, around 3pm, and we got stuck in traffic in the middle of tunnel. In the van was me, the driver, the assistant manager and the still unconscious European Fallow deer.

My job was to stay in the back of the small truck with the deer. It was rush hour, and the traffic inside the tunnel was barely moving. I then noticed the deer starting to wake up. I was now holding a deer that was starting to come out of sedation in the back of a Humane Society truck in the middle of the Detroit-Windsor Tunnel in traffic moving at a snail's pace. I told the officer in the front that we better move faster. *"Tell that to the tunnel traffic"*, he snarled back at me. When we finally reached the U.S. Customs Inspection, they quickly waved us through, the deer becoming more and more alert. We weren't even asked for our ID. Belle Isle was only 12 minutes away. We made it just in time. The prisoner was successfully released to the U.S. authorities.

The Tunnel
(Photo - The Windsor Star)

Built ahead of schedule and under-budget ($24 million, or $300 million in today's dollars), the Detroit-Windsor Tunnel has always been considered a marvel of engineering. Opened with the distant turn of a key by President Herbert Hoover in Washington DC, at midnight on November 3, 1930, it was designed and built by the same firm that developed the Holland Tunnel in New York. The tunnel is a mile long (1.57km), and lies under the waters of the Detroit River, 75' below the surface at the lowest level. 4-5 million vehicle trips pay tolls to the tunnel annually. The City of Windsor owns the Canadian half, a Bermuda based insurance company owns the American half.

not a chickenhawk

The Windsor/Essex County Humane Society handled calls concerning all types of wildlife, like birds, skunks, squirrels, rabbits and opossums. And occasionally domestic livestock. They had (and still have) a great working relationship with Wings Wildlife Rehabilitation. This organization, co-founded by Nancy Phillips from Amherstburg, would usually successfully rehabilitate all manner of wildlife that we sent to them, either brought to us by a member of the public, or rescued by us directly.

Once, a large Red-Tailed Hawk that had been hit by a car was brought into the shelter. It was still alive, but unconscious. Co-worker Steve was carrying the hawk back to the work area. The hawk, which was stunned, woke just when Steve removed one of his hands to open a door. The next thing Steve knew, the hawk had dug its talons into the underside of Steve's wrist. We tried to pry them out, but the more we pulled, the deeper the talons went in. I finally grabbed some pliers and started pulling each talon out individually, the hawk trying furiously to be elsewhere, and Steve bleeding profusely and howling in pain. The inner part of the human wrist has many veins and arteries, and Steve's blood was everywhere. We wrapped his wrist and I transported him to the hospital. After a week off, he came back to work, his wrist still bandaged.

Red-Tailed Hawk (buteo jamaicensis)
Audubon.org

The hawk was rehabilitated and eventually released into the area where it came from, talons intact. Steve fully recovered.

what's the soup?

One of the strangest calls I went on involved Snapping Turtles.

North American Snapping Turtle (*chelydra serpentina*)
(en.wikipedia.org)

The Windsor Tunnel people had notified the Humane Society that an American guy in a truck was being denied entry back into the United States by U.S. Customs, because he didn't have the proper paperwork for the 60 live large Snapping Turtles he had in the back of his truck. I was dispatched to the Canadian entrance to the tunnel and proceeded to a secondary holding area at Canada Customs. I took the gentleman's information. Lucky for me, the snapping turtles were in burlap sacks. I asked him what he was going to do with the turtles. He stated he was going to use them for soup.

I transported the turtles to the shelter and placed them in a large run and watered them down. The next day the man returned with the proper paperwork and was on his way back across the border.

To make a batch of turtle soup.

not goat's head soup

The shelter at times was a temporary home for all manner of livestock. There was one particular goat I remember.

For about 3 weeks, I took care of a young goat that had been brought in. Every day I would bring it food and water, let it outside, clean the pen area, and spend some time with it, like he was one of our dogs. I didn't think he paid any attention to me, that I was just the person he saw every day helping him. Plus, I didn't know a lot about goats. After 3 weeks, the shelter found a good farm for the goat, where he would spend the rest of his life. I happened to be busy when I noticed that they were taking it out of the building to its new life. As soon as the goat saw me, it walked over, and looked right up at me as if to say "Thank You". I patted him on the head and said "*You're very welcome*". The job certainly had its rewards. That one was worth a million.

oh possum wherefore art thou?

The *Opossum*, or *possum*, native to the Southern United States, has been a resident in the Windsor area for the last few decades. My introduction to this marsupial came in the spring of 1984, when I received a call from a lady who was freaking out because there was a "*gigantic rat*" in her backyard shed. We didn't usually go on rat calls because, ordinarily, if you had a rat problem you called the City of Windsor, as they had (still have) a rat extermination program. But because this lady was so worried, I decided to go and check it out.

The opossum is a marsupial of the order Didelphimorphia endemic to the Americas. The largest order of marsupials in the Western Hemisphere, it comprises 103 or more species. Source – Wikipedia

She lived in south Walkerville, close to Memorial Drive, which runs adjacent to the Canadian Pacific

Railway tracks, right in the heart of Windsor. I arrived about 4:30 pm. The lady brought me straight to the shed. I opened the door and sure enough, on a shelf in the upper corner, was a large rodent-looking creature. It opened its mouth to display 2 *rows of teeth,* from front to back, top to bottom. I had never seen an opossum in person before, just a picture, but I knew this wasn't a rat. I figured it probably had gotten there on one of the thousands of trains Windsor gets every year from down south.

I met no resistance as I put it in a transport cage using the catchpole, and into my van. I reassured the lady that she didn't have a rat problem, and now didn't have an opossum problem either.

To tell you the truth the only thing I knew about possums before this was from the *Beverly Hillbillies*.

Copyright CBS Television

who was that masked procryon lotor?

Raccoons, like opossums, are nocturnal. They forage in garbage and gardens at night searching for food. If seen during daylight hours, there is usually something wrong, and they may be sick or injured.

Procryon lotor, aka common raccoon
(pixabay.com)

A motorist called the Humane Society about a racoon stuck in a sewer grate. I arrived at the location on Grand Marais Road just east of Walker Road. Grand Marais Rd. runs alongside Turkey Creek just south of the Chrysler Corporation Property. This waterway is fondly referred to by most Windsorites as the "*Grand Marais Ditch*". I soon saw the raccoon in the grate. It was very young and barely alive, not even strong enough to struggle. I figured it had tried to come out of the sewer and out to the street, but got stuck. I pried it from the sewer lid but it died in a matter of minutes. I shined my flashlight into the sewer and noticed there was a mother racoon and two babies, stuck, down about 6 feet. I thought they may have got in the sewer from a pipe which led from the creek, and couldn't get back out. I called the city

Public Works for assistance in opening the grate. They opened it about 20 minutes later. Now I could use my catch pole. Todd, the city guy, held my flashlight while I attempted to catch this poor trapped raccoon family. Time and time again they would escape into a little area which I couldn't reach. Finally after about an hour and a half, we got all three of them in cages.

They seemed pretty healthy, so I released them into the Devonwood Conservation Area, about a mile and a half away. This conservation area is owned by the City of Windsor and consists of a large wooded area and manicured trails. It was the closest appropriate place to release them. According to Humane Society policy, animals such as these raccoons had to be taken to a suitable area closest to where they were found.

skunks – great, just great (apologies to john prine)

Skunks posed a big problem for us, for obvious reasons.

Of all the skunks that I had to pick up, maybe a dozen or so, only a few didn't spray. Whether they were sick, injured or hit by a car, they were usually still strong enough to deploy their unique defense mechanism.

Generally, when I approached a skunk, I would try to handle it from the front, because you don't want to be at the back or business end of the skunk when it lifts its tail up, arches its back legs and releases its charming scent. No matter what happens, front or back, your clothes and everything else was going to smell and need to be tossed. Who am I kidding? I have a feeling everybody knows this.

Following the general skunk protocol, once an injured one was picked up and placed in a cage, I would have to bring it to the shelter, euthanize it, and then place it in our freezer. The following day I was not too popular, because the whole shelter would have a foul odour. You could say *"It smelled like a dead skunk in the middle of the road, stinking to high heaven" - Loudon Wainwright III, "Dead Skunk").*

Common striped skunk (*Mephitis mephitis*)
(Photo en.wikipedia.org)

"We saw also a couple of Zorrillos, or skunks—odious animals, which are far from uncommon. In general appearance, the Zorrillo resembles a polecat, but it is rather larger and much thicker in proportion. Conscious of its power, it roams by day about the open plain, and fears neither dog nor man. If a dog is urged to the attack, its courage is instantly checked by a few drops of the fetid oil, which brings on violent sickness and running at the nose".

Excerpt - Charles Darwin's Voyage of the Beagle:

snake in the grass – two snake mistakes

Every now and again in our line of work we would come across animals of the more exotic variety. Snakes, iguanas and lizards are some of the non-indigenous creatures that people had for pets. My knowledge of these creatures was very limited. This limitation came to the forefront early in my career, when I received a call one night about a snake hanging around on someone's front porch.

I attended the call at a home in the Remington Park area of Windsor, basically right in the middle of the city. It was in the summertime about 10 pm. When I got to the address, the homeowner took me to the spot where the snake was located. It was about 3 – 4 feet in length. _Mistake #1_. It looked like an ordinary fox snake, the _Carolinian_ kind commonly found in our area, so I put it in a cage and, _Mistake #2_, released it into a grassy field adjacent to the Grand Marais Drain.

Early the next day someone called the Humane Society and said there was a snake sunning itself on their back porch. I hadn't started work yet, so another officer went to the address and picked up what turned out to be the very same snake. He correctly identified it as a _young python snake_. When I came into work, my first call of the day was to the Manager's Office. I was reprimanded for failing to correctly identify the potentially dangerous snake, and told to always ask for help if I wasn't sure about any call I was going on. To make matters worse, _The Windsor Star_ found out about the mix-up, and ran a story about it. Not the first time a snake had gotten someone in trouble.

Eastern Fox snake
(wildlife.ohiodnr.gov)

Burmese Rock Python
(Smithsoniannationalzoo.si.edu)

Could *you* tell the difference?

About two months later, the Humane Society received a call from a resident who said there was a large snake in her home. This time I was prepared – I brought my partner Steve along on the call. When we arrived at her home in the downtown area of the city, the resident, a lady in her 30's, was scared and freaked out. She said the last time she saw the snake, it was near the cold air return of her furnace. Steve and I proceeded to check the whole house from top to bottom, hoping to come across the snake. We spent almost an hour looking, with no luck.

So we thought the only place it could be was somewhere in the furnace duct system. It was summer, so the furnace wasn't operating. It was one of those old fashioned oil furnaces, with round ducts leading everywhere. We opened up a few of the ducts and shone our flashlights inside, but nothing appeared. We were about to give up when Steve noticed a smaller duct that was on a peculiar angle that we couldn't see inside or reach with our catch pole. He came up with a brilliant idea. He grabbed a fishing rod that was nearby, took it apart, ran a rope through it. He then reached into the small duct with his improvised nifty homemade snare, and magically pulled out a 4 foot long fox snake, which was quietly released into the wild, without incident.

I was glad Steve was with me that day. The homeowner felt totally relieved that this creature was out of her house.

This time, we didn't make the newspaper.

professional dancer, nice interpretation

As some of you may have heard, exotic dancers occasionally use snakes as part of their show. The Humane Society was alerted one day about a certain dancer who was using a Boa Constrictor as part of her act at "*The Booby Trap*", a strip club that was very strategically located on Drouillard Road. The club was surrounded at the time by the Big Three auto factories: General Motors, Ford, and Chrysler. Location, location, and location.

Her show started at 9 p.m. Four of us went, two of our officers dressed in plain clothes, with our boss Marilyn and me (in uniform) stationed in the Humane Society van parked in front of the club. We were concerned that we might have to remove the snake, but the dancer just did her routine with the snake around her neck, didn't abuse or frighten the snake or use it in any particularly perverse way during her act, this confirmed by our two lucky undercover Humane Society officers. After watching the show, the two officers confirmed that the snake had a proper cage and was provided with all necessities. All in the line of duty at the Humane Society.

While sitting there in the van with Marilyn, I listened to her running commentary on the men that were going in and out of the club. That was pretty funny, I have to say.

a wily coyote

On my very last day ever on the afternoon shift, we received a call about a possible coyote in the Willistead Park area. Blake and I attended. Sure enough, we observed a large coyote wandering in the park in the heart of the city, no doubt looking for food, and likely got in through one of the open gates in the iron fencing surrounding the property.

Willistead Park is an historical municipal park in the Walkerville area of Windsor. It contains Willistead Manor, which was built by Hiram Walker for his son Edward, and named after his other son Willis. Today it is used as an event centre. Every Christmas it is open to the public for tours. In the 50's and 60's it was a Public Library which I visited many times as a kid. Our editor took art classes there from Mr. Saltmarche.

Blake and I watched closely as the coyote wandered into St Mary's Gate, immediately north of the park. We thought we had lost it, but then I noticed it had crouched down in a neighbour's backyard, probably just trying to hide. While we were keeping our eye on the coyote, the police and our veterinarian arrived, armed with the tranquilizer rifle and the necessary drugs. In a short time the coyote noticed the attention it was garnering, and started to run back into the park. Our best chance to use the gun was in the corner of the park. Once there, a single shot of the tranquilizer gun was enough to slow down and immobilize the probably completely confused coyote. We placed the totally out-of-it animal in the van, and with assistance from our veterinarian, drove to the outskirts of town and waited for the coyote to revive. Once the vet examined the animal, it was released into a wooded area. Problem solved. A good way to end my final afternoon shift.

Canis latrans – coyote
(photo - mass.gov)

"Coyotes rarely pose a danger to people. They are often curious, and very used to people so don't show a lot of fear or wariness. If you unexpectedly encounter a coyote in close quarters wave your arms, shout, and even throw objects to show it that you mean business. Most coyotes won't take more than a second to high-tail it out of there if you put on an aggressive display. If a coyote is in your yard you can follow the same tips, as well as banging on a pot with a spoon or spraying them with a garden hose".

-Windsor/Essex County Humane Society Website

CHAPTER FIVE – ears to you, mister – the troubling story of AK that has a happy ending

This terrible story emanating out of Windsor received national attention. On Friday May 11, 2007 Windsor/Essex County Humane Society got an anonymous tip about a dog whimpering and sitting on a balcony of a second floor apartment in the 3400 block of Sandwich Street.

The Humane Society attended with the Windsor Police. There they found a German shepherd-rottweiller cross that was bleeding from the area where his ears had been. Both ears had been cut off, possibly by a knife or saw. When the owner of the dog was questioned, he first stated that he had just recently got the dog from a friend. He claimed later that he bought the dog, the ears had already been removed. Then he later said this was the result of a dog fight.

AK and me at the Humane Society
(Photo Canadian Press)

Nevertheless, he quickly signed ownership of the dog over to the Humane Society, and AK was immediately taken to a veterinary clinic for treatment. My co-worker Nancy later learned that the Humane Society had been to this address a few times before over complaints about a dog being abused. The Society also received calls from people who had seen the owner with AK in the last few months, contradicting his story about just receiving the dog recently. Nancy was the Field Operations Manager for the Humane Society and she built the case against the owner. With the help of the O.S.P.C.A., charges were laid.

The owner of this excellent German shepherd-rottweiller cross was convicted and sentenced to 90 days in jail for cutting the puppy's ears off. He was later sentenced to prison again, for another completely unrelated offence. I guess the story got around in the jail, because another prisoner reportedly gave him his comeuppance and actually bit part of one of the guy's own ears off, a lá what Mike Tyson did to Evander Holyfield on June 28, 1977 at the MGM Grand in Las Vegas.

I took care of this wonderful dog while it was housed at the Humane Society. It was very friendly when I was first saw it, even with the large bandage wrapped around his ears and head. I spent extra time with it as the dog needed to be carefully watched for complications, and just as important, to help this canine regain its trust in people. We were there to help AK, the name given to him by the idiot offender. Maybe he named the dog after the AK – 47 assault rifle, which wouldn't surprise me.

The national attention this incident gained resulted in people from all over the country looking to adopt AK. The story prompted changes to the relevant legislation, not just in Ontario, but in other provinces. People were angered at the relatively light 90 day jail sentence that he got.

He was adopted by some very nice people.

Owner charged with cutting off puppy's ears

Caroline Alphonso Education Reporter, The Globe and Mail
Published June 8, 2007 Updated April 25, 2018

The owner of a German shepherd-rottweiller puppy that was found on an apartment balcony last month with its ears cut off has been charged with animal cruelty.

AK made national headlines after the SPCA found him whimpering on a Windsor, Ont., balcony with his ears sliced off, allegedly an attempt to make the dog look more menacing.

Rony Salman, 29, of Windsor, faces seven charges, including willfully causing unnecessary pain, suffering and injury by cutting the dog's ears, failing to take the dog to a vet and neglecting to care for the injured dog. He is to appear in court Aug. 13.

Despite his traumatizing ordeal, AK has maintained a happy demeanour. His hearing hasn't been affected because there was no internal damage.

The Windsor/Essex County Humane Society has received 13 adoption applications and are in the process of selecting a family for the puppy.

AK's ordeal prompted the Ontario government to look at reviewing its animal-cruelty act, and animal lovers to demand changes to Canada's Criminal Code. Critics charge that inadequate animal cruelty laws mean that those found guilty could serve only a maximum of six months in jail *and/or receive a $2,000 fine, as well as a two-year ban on owning an animal.*

Hugh Coghill, Ontario SPCA acting chief inspector, said charges would have been brought much sooner if the dog had been injured in other provinces, such as British Columbia or Alberta. Those provinces have enacted tougher legislation that could ban people from ever owning an animal again if they caused or permitted an animal to be in distress.

In Ontario, however, only those breeding and selling dogs and cats are committing a provincial offence if they don't follow standards. Owners who abuse their animals are punishable under the Criminal Code.

CHAPTER SIX – out of control puppy mill nightmare

Is it any wonder I'm not crazy?
Is it any wonder I'm sane at all?
Is it any wonder I'm not a criminal?
Is it any wonder I'm not in jail?

- **Styx, "Too Much Time on My Hands"**
-

"The breeder who is not willing to give some time to the puppies should let

someone else do the breeding and puppy raising. There are enough poorly adjusted dogs in the world now that did not get the people-care they needed while they were puppies. This is where the so-called "puppy mills" are totally negligent. The people who operate these mills have a large number of female dogs whose only function is to produce puppies for profit and who are often kept in cages, boxes or other very small areas. This so-called "breeder" has no understanding of the needs of the dog and does not realize the damage done to a pup's personality by giving it no socialization during the first eight weeks. It is not only extreme cruelty to keep the parent dogs in such confining isolation, but it is also cruel to the puppies to deny them the socialization they must have if they are to adjust to living with people as they grow up"

Rutherford and Neil, *How to Raise a Puppy You Can Live With*, Alpine Publications, 1981, 1992

In 1992, the Humane Society was alerted by the Essex O.P.P. about a possible neglect situation involving a large number of dogs living in a house in the county just south of Windsor. The property was listed for sale, and a couple that had been interested were repulsed by the odour coming from the house as they walked by it.

A number of us went to investigate. I immediately observed hundreds of flies in each window, so I knew this was going to be bad, and I was right. The owner let us in, and we were all shocked – there's no other word for it. The house was full of *dozens* of small dogs. I was almost gagged by the stench.

There was no one actually living there, just what looked like 60 to 70 dogs, mainly white or tan lhasa-apso and cock-a-poo types. The dogs definitely did not appear to be socialized. Some had physical deformities. The floors were filled with feces and urine stains. Some of the dogs' fur was so matted we couldn't determine the sex. Some were nursing pups, and some were about to give birth. In a house next door, owned by the same people, we found another 60 or 70 dogs in the same horrible condition. The windows were covered up, blocking any sunlight for the dogs.

This was a nightmare.

Our shelter manager, Marilyn came with us. She ordered that all these dogs were to be removed as soon as possible. She said this was the worst case of neglect that she had ever seen in her time at the Humane Society.

The owner tearfully handed the dogs over to us. A few days later, we removed more of this woman's other dogs from an animal clinic out in the county in Tilbury, all in similar terrible condition. Most were very sick, had not been vaccinated, had injuries from fighting, or showed physical deformities likely from inter-breeding. Some were badly crippled. The fleas had made many of them anemic. Most of these dogs did not even know how to eat out of a bowl.

Only a few were actually healthy.

In all, the Humane Society removed 320 dogs. It was then one of the largest seizure of dogs in Canadian history, and quite possibly the largest. Brian Denham, then Executive Director of the O.S.P.C.A., stated that he had never heard of a case of neglect that equalled what was found that day on County Road 9 in Essex County.

We used all of our vehicles to transport these dogs to the shelter. The shelter was already full, so their arrival meant they were placed everywhere in the building, including the hallways and offices. Fifty had to be euthanized on the spot, they were in such bad condition. Our veterinarian examined the rest of the dogs carefully and realized that because of their poor health, most were too far gone and could not be saved, let alone adopted out. Days later, and with no alternative, he re-examined the rest of the dogs, and directed many more of them to be put down. I was the assistant. In two days the veterinarian and I euthanized 150 dogs, eighty on one day, seventy the next. Not socialized with humans, many of them tried to bite during this unsettling process.

As you can imagine, all this was very depressing for me and everyone else at the shelter. It was, however, totally unavoidable. We had to do what we had to do. And in spite of all this, some of the dogs were actually saved and adopted out.

I don't know what ever happened to the dog owner. I wonder if she ever has nightmares about this, because I sure do.

CHAPTER SEVEN – the guy with the tattoos

In the mid-1980s, I was working the night shift when I got a call – a page, actually - about a dog being abused. In those days on the 4 to midnight shift, I worked calls dispatched directly from the office until 8pm. After 8pm with no one in the building except me, I would get my calls and instructions from a pager worn on my belt (this was the 1980s, after all). Complaints from the public about animal abuse or neglect or other emergencies after 8pm would go to an answering service who would leave a "page" for me. These pages might or might not have given me the name and telephone number of the person making the complaint, further details like the description and location of an animal being abused, address, description of the animal etc. No two pages were the same. This was just before the advent of the cell phone, so any telephone calls to be made by me to say, the police or an emergency veterinarian, required the insertion of coins into a pay phone. Have I now dated myself enough?

On that night this particular page told me a man was beating his dog, and directed me to a particular townhouse-type unit at a low income Windsor Housing project on Millen St on the west side of Windsor - a neighbourhood well-known to police. Usually when I neared a house or an apartment where a particular problem stemmed from, in the projects as we called them, I could pretty well tell where to go exactly, as the place where the problem arose was almost always the worst-kept house or unit. This unit was no exception. Old newspapers, garbage, dirty windows, badly smudged grimy front door.

I arrived at the row housing building at around 9 pm. It was getting dark, and this was in the muggy heat of a typical Windsor summer. There was lots of noise from neighbouring units – stereos and TVs, people, talking, laughing and arguing, babies crying. I quickly identified the townhouse in question, it fitting the description I expected.

In my Humane Society uniform, I knocked on the door. A man in his thirties answered. I identified myself as a Humane Society Officer and told him that we had received a complaint about someone at that address who was heard beating his dog. I asked him if there was a dog there. He said there was.

I told him I would have to see the dog. He went inside and then came out with his dog. With the porch light on and also using my flashlight, I visually examined the dog, a young lab cross, still a puppy, and then felt every part of the dog's legs, belly, chest, neck, tail, and face, looking for any signs of abuse, like cuts, lumps or tender spots. The dog appeared OK. At my request, we then went inside. I asked the man, who was on the other side of the room, to call the dog over to him so I could see the dog's reaction. He complied. The dog initially hesitated a little, but then went over to him. I next asked him to raise his hand toward the dog. The dog cowered a little. This told me that he may have done something to the dog, that there might be something to the complaint. I then asked if there had been a problem with the dog.

He nervously explained that he needed to discipline the dog for chewing on furniture. I explained that sometimes there is a thin line between discipline and abuse and warned him in no uncertain terms that it was against the law to cross the line and abuse or harm any animal for whatever reason. Without denying or admitting anything, he assured me that he would never, ever, abuse or harm his pet.

While this was going on, I heard a man's angry voice from two units down, meaning business, and coming in our direction, *"What's going on over there?"*

I looked over and saw a very big, muscular, real mean-looking biker type guy in his 30s – black boots, shaved head, tattoos on his arms and neck, black t shirt – a dude not to be messed with – stomping angrily towards me. Not knowing what to expect next, I thought to myself, *"Oh sh*t - two against one - against me. Now I'm in for it"*.

Up went my heart rate as I experienced the unmistakable fight-flight response to danger, men's version, and I'm not just referring to dilated pupils. This guy had me real scared.

He came up to the porch and looked at me and then at the guy I was investigating, and in a loud voice, he told the man, *"If you don't listen to this Humane Society guy and do what he tells you, three things are going to happen. One, I'm going to beat the **% out of you. Two, I'm going to %*% *your wife, and three, I'm going to *&$% you!"*

I quietly concluded to myself that Mr. Biker was the complainant. And that on the inside he liked animals. Now it was the dog owner who was worried. It was now two against one alright, myself and the biker vs the dog beater. I was greatly relieved, to say the least. The man went out of his way to make sure that I and my new friend were fully convinced of his innocence, that he was sorry, that it wouldn't happen again. So I left.

I'm sure he never laid another beating, or anything like it, on the dog. Or any other dog.

CHAPTER EIGHT – cats (not the musical) - cat on a hot windsor roof

Felis catis – common house cat
(photo by S. Vesala)

Felix the Cat
(fathom.com)

Did you know this? We didn't

Cats are solitary independent night roamers. More so if they're not spayed or neutered.

The Humane Society took in thousands of stray cats every year when I was there. This number went down considerably in the later years after the opening of the "Spay and Neuter" clinic at the Humane Society in 2011. That was really something.

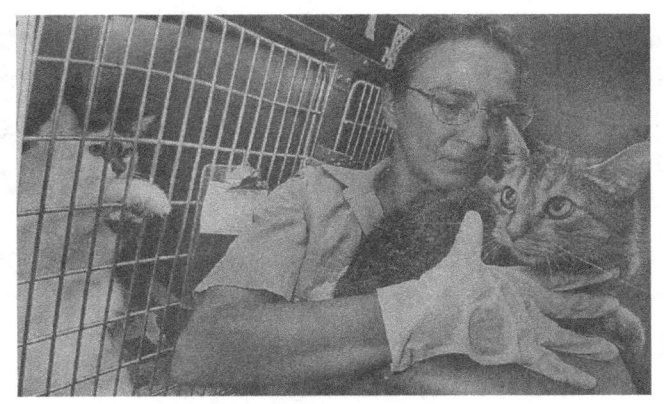

The late Jeanne Trepanier
(Photo Scott Webster / Windsor Star)

Cats sometimes end up in the most unimaginable and difficult places, like vehicle engines. Or up live hydro poles. Unlike racoons, cats are unable to climb down backwards, so when a cat is up a tree, it meows and meows and meows, almost always prompting neighbours to call the Humane Society, to do whatever it takes to get the cat down, no matter how difficult or dangerous. *"It's your job"*, we would hear a lot.

With the help of a long neighbourhood ladder, I could usually get the cat down, but this wasn't always easy because it required holding the cat by the scruff with one hand and manoeuvring down the ladder with the other hand. Many times it would be raining or blowing (or both) which made things even more difficult. After a while the Humane Society made friends with a lighting maintenance worker who had a truck with a hydraulic lift. This guy helped us out many times, and we were very grateful, as were the cats and their owners.

We once received a call about a cat stuck on a very steep, two storey roof of a house on Cadillac Street, just opposite the Ford Motor Company Franklin Street gate, on the east side of the city. I arrived about 4:30 pm. I had the extension ladder. Our assistant manager Verne was there with me, to hold the ladder. Manager Marilyn was also there. When I reached the roof, I noticed how sloped up it was. The cat, a brown tabby, was at the roof's peak. Getting to the top was not that difficult, even though it was steep. Just as I got close, the cat went down the other side and jumped down onto the front porch overhang, and then made his way down the side of the porch, and quickly skedaddled. Now I was on the roof near the peak, all by my sorry self. The way down the very steep roof was going to be difficult, and right then and there I realized I was afraid of heights. I froze. I thought I would never make it down from that roof. Eventually, I crawled backwards very slowly, and made it to the ladder. All in front of the neighbours, a co-worker, and management.

The cat was long gone, all nine lives intact.

down the drain

One Saturday in the summer, I received a call about a kitten stuck in a storm sewer drain. Somehow, the 3-4 week old small kitten had fallen down the storm drain in the back area of a motel. This motel, on Howard Avenue near the expressway, was well-run by a nice Windsor family. The owners were Humane Society supporters, and friends to all animals. These nice people had helped many stray cats over the years. I got there about 2 pm. They anxiously showed me where the cat had fallen. I could hear the kitten, but just barely. I estimated it was about 5 feet down in the storm drain. At first I tried our catch pole which could reach there easily. The pipe leading down to the drain was around 4 inches diameter so there was some room to maneuver. I tried and tried without success, but I could only blindly feel around. This was frustrating because I could faintly hear the kitten, but I couldn't do anything. To make things worse, I received an unrelated emergency call about a cat that had been hit by a car. Emergency calls like that always took priority. While on this new call, I was still bothered that I couldn't help the kitten in the storm drain. When I finished with the other cat, which had only a minor injury, I returned to the motel.

This time I started digging around the 4 inch storm drain pipe and dug down far enough to where I could remove one of the pipes, which allowed me better access. I stuck my arm down into the drain and I soon felt the kitten, but it wasn't allowing me to grab it. Finally, with the tips of two fingers, I managed to grasp the scruff of the little kitten and pulled it out. It took two attempts, but the 4 week old kitten was now free. It was a good thing too, because later on it poured with rain and the kitten would have drowned.

cats, more cats, stray cat blues

Throughout the 1980's and 90's, thousands of cats were housed at our shelter. Sometimes 5,000 a year. I'm serious. Most were strays brought in by the public, not by us, because there was (still is) no law prohibiting cats to run at large. The Humane Society would only pick up cats that were sick or injured.

You really can't run down a cat like you can a dog, which also is difficult. They are much too elusive. And street-wise feral (wild) cats live their lives on the streets, and are very difficult to capture, even when injured or sick. They seem to like their circumstances. A nasty street cat bit me so severely once that I needed stitches. My arms show plenty of cat battle scars from more than a few unfriendly big tom cats with huge jowls, loud hisses, and un-manicured long front and back claws.

I remember one tom cat that I brought to the on-duty veterinarian. It was huge, about twenty pounds, and it had a serious vicious attitude. The veterinarian looked it over and said, *"This cat has been fooling around with half of the cats in Windsor, and fighting with the other half"*. A big time alley cat. We had no choice but to put it down. At least it had fun while it was alive.

cucamongas crazy cat ladies calling us names

Like other Humane Societies, we would occasionally receive complaints about eccentric, over-the-top cat hoarders. We got a complaint about numerous cats in a lady's house on Cabana Rd., just east of Howard Ave, very near the shelter. The City of Windsor by-law (*Ed. - see addendum for current by-law*) in those days only allowed for 2 cats per household.

This woman had 12 cats inside her house. We explained the by-law to her, and she reluctantly but angrily agreed to give up ten cats. The only problem was that they were all over the house and none of them was very friendly or socialized, so we had to round up the cats without causing any damage. The lady refused to help in any way. After an hour of chaos, we finally had the cats safe and sound in cages. The still mad lady called Marilyn our manager, saying she didn't have to "*send in the storm troopers*".

We got a call about another cat lady located on Park St. just east of Sandwich St. in Amherstburg. It was the same scenario as the previous call, i.e. we had to round up about 20 cats and remove them to the shelter in Windsor. Again, all of the cats were indoors. It took all day.

In the early 2000's we received yet another one of these calls. The location was in Leamington on a road just east of County Rd. 33, very close to Point Pelee National Park.

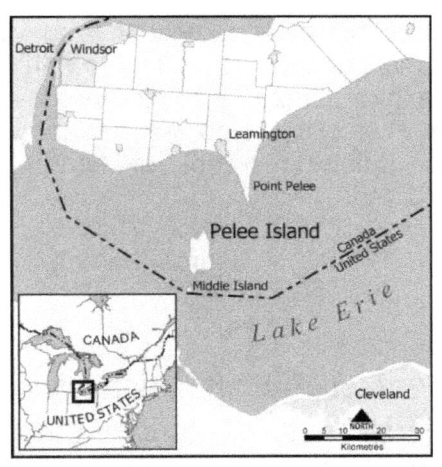

(en.wikipedia.org)

Point Pelee National Park (Lat. 41.96.28°N, Long. 82.51.84°W) is a favourite for people, including bird-watchers, from all over the world. Designated as #66 out of 100, in Dominic Couzen's *Top 100 Birding Sites of the World*.(2009 University of California Press), it is the most southern point in Canada's mainland. The park hosts over 360 bird types, as well as the vital Monarch Butterfly, many of which stop to rest at Point Pelee, when migrating, in both directions. First Nations lived there 6000 years ago. In fact, it is said to be unceded first nations land, due to a slip-up by the British (no Chippewa signatures on the treaty). Designated a National Park in 1918, the park is 1,113 hectares (3,860 acres) in area. World famous Canadian conservationist Jack Miner (1865-1944), grew up in Essex, began as a trapper and hunter, but later devoted his life to helping migratory birds, pioneering the use of identity tags (50,000 ducks, 40,000 geese). A conservative, religious man, he wrote *Jack Miner and the Birds* (Amazon.ca), which is still in print. He opened his sanctuary, *The Jack*

Miner Bird Sanctuary, located in Kingsville near the national park he had a lot to do with opening up. This bird sanctuary is still there. *National Wildlife Week* is celebrated every year in Canada during the week of April 10, Jack Miner's birthday.

Source (partial)-Wikipedia

Me, my co-worker Tim, and our assistant manager Ron, attended. Ron had a dark mustache. He went to speak to the lady, but she refused to talk to him. Instead, she turned to Tim and me and said *"I'm not talking to him. He has a Nazi face."* We looked at each other and laughed. She didn't laugh.

To be fair, these were all strong-willed ladies who thought they were doing the right thing. And they did love their cats. Just too many of them at once.

yet even more cat stories

I was dispatched one Saturday to check on a cat that was caught in a "humane trap" in a fenced-in factory compound, one of many like businesses located along Rhodes Dr. in a big industrial zone in Windsor. I brought Jim, a part-timer, with me.

A Humane Trap sold at Canadian Tire
(canadiantire.ca)

We got there and found the factory closed and nobody on site. We called dispatch to see if they could locate any officials from the factory. No luck. We followed the fence toward the back of the compound, where we observed a brown tabby adult cat in the trap on the other side of the fence. These traps don't hurt cats, only lock them in. When the animal enters and steps on a trip plate, the door closes and locks behind it.

We were absolutely not going to leave that cat in there until possibly Monday morning when the factory re-opened. Since the fence was about 8 feet high, I nominated Jim to climb it and retrieve the trap with the cat inside. He went to the trap, and a minute later handed it off over the fence to me. I placed it in our van. Back at the shelter with the cat, we set it up with food, water and a blanket. It was hungry.

We returned to the factory and placed the empty trap back over the fence, and set the trap up in case there were any other stray cats there. We checked the trap the next day, a Sunday. It was empty. I left an official note on the front door of the factory explaining what had occurred, advising they should check the trap at <u>least</u> once a day.

fleas and thank you

An elderly woman called us once, concerned about some neighborhood stray cats she had been feeding. Co-worker Verne and I arrived at her home on Felix Ave on the west side. Most of the houses there are "war-time houses", the ones that resemble *Monopoly©* markers.

The lady said the 2 cats were in the basement and that one of them looked very bad. We went down and saw a black and white adult cat lying on the floor, the other black adult cat sitting nearby. The black and white cat was dead. Upon further inspection I noticed it was infested with fleas. I had never seen that many fleas on any animal before. The poor cat had probably died from blood loss. The next thing I noticed was a large group of fleas quickly springing from the dead cat to me. Verne experienced the same thing. There were hundreds of fleas all over us. We quickly covered the dead cat and put it in a cage and then put the black cat in the other cage. This cat was also thoroughly flea infested. We raced outside and started frantically jumping around trying to shake the fleas off. Somewhat miraculously, a woman from the house next door suddenly came at us with Black Flag insect spray and started spraying our clothing down, which was welcome indeed. We quickly thanked her and left, scratching ourselves all the way back to the shelter.

CHAPTER NINE – don't try this at home

One day in 1984, I was dispatched to an address on Moy Avenue near downtown Windsor on a possible animal abuse call. The complainant had advised the office that he had heard what sounded like a dog yelping in severe pain, coming from his next door neighbour's garage.

Upon arrival to a reasonably well-kept middle class home, I rang the doorbell. I identified myself to the gentleman who came to the door, said I was from the Windsor Humane Society, and advised him that we had heard from a neighbour that there was a dog yelping that sounded like it was in distress. Pursuant to procedure, I asked to see the dog in question.

The man went back into the house and soon returned with a white German shepherd type dog, male, about 6 or 7 months old. After looking the dog over I noticed there was blood, some dried, some fresh, on the underside of the dog's backend. I asked the guy, a man in his 30's, what had happened to the dog, and to explain the blood on the dog's underside. He told me that he had neutered his dog - *himself*. More than a little alarmed, I asked him how he did it.

He stated that he had neutered the dog with hand-held *rosebush clippers!* He went on to say that his family used this method to neuter pigs on their farm. I explained that we were not on a farm, and that castration had to be done by a veterinarian in a clinic. I then proceeded to remove the dog, telling, not asking him, *"This dog has to go to the vet immediately"*.

Without argument or protest, he agreed to release the dog to me. I took it straight to our veterinary clinic, where the vet conducted a thorough examination. I gathered all the facts, took pictures of the dog, and obtained a statement from the owner and the complainant. We got a Medical Report from the veterinarian. We had decided to lay charges for this unacceptable instance of serious animal abuse.

This case went to Windsor Provincial Court, the charge being animal cruelty under the then provincial statute. I testified, telling the judge what I had seen and what the accused had told me, showed the pictures, the statements, and the report. After hearing my testimony, and getting submissions from the prosecutor and the guy's lawyer, the judge found the man guilty, but determined that the penalty *would only be a $150.00 fine*! The judge did rule that the man would lose ownership of the dog, and so we got the dog. The Humane Society put the young shepherd up for adoption and he quickly ended up with a nice family. (Really. The dog really ended up with a nice young family. Just not on a farm).

The ludicrous, paltry fine meted out by the judge here was certainly not much of a penalty for inflicting this kind of pain on an innocent animal.

88

CHAPTER TEN – emergency work – that's some catch that catch 22

The most difficult, but at times the most rewarding part of my job as a Humane Society Officer, was handling emergencies involving all animals. I dealt mostly with dogs and cats hit by cars, giving them first-aid, and transporting them safely to a veterinarian. Any animal struck by a vehicle almost always had to be seen by a vet, for fear of internal injuries and bleeding, broken bones and cartilage, or head trauma. Our Humane Society vans were classified as 2nd class ambulances, which meant we could speed a bit, but only safely, and never in residential areas. If I had a critically injured dog or cat I, I would push it, but only when safe to do so.

A predecessor
(Photo Windsor Star)

In the early 80's, there were no 24 hour animal emergency clinics in Windsor. The Humane Society had arrangements with local veterinary clinics to handle our injured or sick animals. When I picked one up, I paged the veterinarian on call and he or she would open up their clinic and deal with the situation at hand. Injured wildlife, like rabbits, skunks, opossums and birds, were brought to the shelter. Under directions from our veterinarian, we would, depending on the severity of the case, put the very sick or injured ones down ourselves. I learned a lot from each veterinarian I worked with, and they never hesitated to share their knowledge and expertise.

Our roads, expressways and highways, with ever increasing traffic mixed with impatient drivers, can be very dangerous for *all* animals. They don't co-exist together. No law says you have to stop after you strike an animal, be it a cat, dog or wildlife. Most people do stop and feel very bad, if not traumatized, about hitting an innocent animal with their vehicles. But, by law, with some exceptions, the drivers don't have to brake, avoid or stop, unless it is a large animal, like a moose or a horse or an elephant. And if they do brake for an animal and cause a pileup, they can very well be held liable in a civil court. It's a Catch 22, really.

Letting a dog loose can cause harm or death to it. Motor vehicle accidents occurring when drivers swerve to avoid these dogs on streets and highways can result in injury and loss of life to humans.

E.C. Row Expressway in Windsor, a busy four-lane divided cross-town east-west highway, is a particularly bad place for our animal friends to be roaming on. The often exceeded legal speed limit is 100 kph/60mph. I'll hazard a guess and say at least 10 dogs or cats, and some wildlife, are killed each and every year by cars or trucks on "E.C. Row". Flanked by a mix of residential, commercial and industrial areas, cement batching plants, sprinkled with places of worship of many denominations, it is cross-section of the city itself, dogs and cats included. It crosses major arteries like Lauzon, Walker, Dougall, and Huron Church Rd. Look to the north and you see the awesome Detroit downtown about 6 kilometres (3 ½ miles) away.

Detroit Skyline from Windsor
(Photo S. Vesala)

Stunning at day or night, the Detroit skyline is a landmark to most people in Windsor and Essex County, who love living next to Detroit, Michigan, a great town, although you do need to know your way around. Every day, 12,000 Canadians commute to Detroit from Windsor, through the tunnel or across the bridge, to go to work one mile away in Detroit. A bus from Windsor goes directly to major league hockey, baseball, basketball and football games, all right downtown in the spiffy new entertainment district of the City of Detroit. About 4.3 million people live in the Detroit Metropolitan area. 330,000 people live in the Windsor-Essex County area. 5.9 million live in Metro-Toronto, not that anybody cares. The last time the Leafs won the Stanley Cup, TV was mostly in black and white.

I was working the dayshift on a Saturday in or about 1985 when I received a call from dispatch about dogs – plural – that had been struck by a car on E.C. Row Expressway, near where it crosses just east of Howard Avenue, the busiest part of the expressway.

When I arrived on the scene I met a very distraught woman who had pulled her car over at the side of the expressway. I then noticed that there were 3 dogs in the median. Two of the dogs were not moving, the third barely moving. She explained that she was driving along and all three dogs just ran out in front of her. She said she simply *could not* avoid hitting them, and I believed her. This nice person went on to say that one of the dogs was in front and the other two dogs were chasing the first one. Apparently the first dog was a female and was being chased by two males. I later determined that none of the dogs had been spayed or neutered. The lady felt really bad and was crying at the side of the road.

I placed all 3 dogs into my truck, 2 of which had already died. The third was still alive – but barely breathing. I transported this one as quickly as possible to our Veterinarian. By the time I reached the clinic, which was only a matter of minutes, the third dog had died. None of the dogs had any form of identification.

Just three unlucky strays, I guess. And another bad day at work for me that I can't forget.

CHAPTER ELEVEN – abandoned run, run, run, run, runaway dogs

People would drive to remote areas, and simply drop off dogs for good. Abandonment of an animal being against the law, many of these heartless people often just dumped their dogs on the sly at an area in the city's west end called Brighton Beach, a secluded area in the west side, popular for dog drop-off. We called it "*Dogpatch*".

Many times the dogs would stay where they had been dumped, waiting for their master to return.

These were good faithful dogs, with cruel and irresponsible owners. This always both broke our hearts and angered us at the same time.

In 1988 I received a call about a dog loose on Highway #3 in front of St. Clair College, the large community college in Windsor. It serves about 10,000 students, local and international. (I actually went there, studying journalism, or *gerbalism*, as we called it). I saw the dog running loose on the part of the highway near the college and drove right up to it, but I had to be very careful not to chase the dog into the four lanes of oncoming traffic. I got out of my van and tried to coax the dog, hoping it would listen and come over to me. Remember, you can't outrun a dog, and if I couldn't gain the dog's trust and physically capture it, my next approach would be to try to get the dog off the highway and out of danger.

I managed to get it into a field across from the college, but the problem was the shepherd-type dog kept running back to the median of the highway, which may have been where the thoughtless owner had dropped it off. After many attempts to remove the dog from the danger, I realized that I was putting my own life in jeopardy. Cars, as usual, weren't slowing down, even with my hazard lights on and the van dome light flashing.

When the dog, still in the median, suddenly ran into the northbound lane, it was immediately struck by a panel van, doing the then 80 kph/50 mph speed limit. I was horrified as I watched the dog fly 30 feet into the air and land on the highway. I immediately went to the dog and removed him off the road. The force from the impact killed the dog on the spot. A dog's loyalty to its owner is stronger than any human loyalty, and this was most likely the reason why this dog kept returning to the spot where he had been dropped off, innocently waiting for its master to return. Dropping dogs off like this endangers innocent people's lives, made my job very dangerous many, many times, and is very much against the law.

A similar situation happened on the freight train tracks directly behind the Humane Society. This area has double tracks, and is part of the American-owned Conrail System, headquartered in Philadelphia, PA. The busy tracks lead to the little-known rail tunnel under the less than one-mile wide Detroit River, from Canada to Detroit and beyond.

My partner Nancy and I were sent to check on the situation. At the scene we saw a female dog with her two puppies dangerously near the tracks. The female black and tan female was a mixed shepherd, one puppy a black and tan, the other a beautiful white shepherd. The puppies were about 10 weeks old. The three dogs were in-between both sets of tracks. Again, the owner of the dogs likely had simply dropped the dogs near there to get rid of them. Not knowing the train schedules, we had to move as fast as we could. We tried to gain the mother's trust to do this, but the three dogs, mother and pups, kept avoiding us, returning to the area where they had been dropped off. Before we knew it there was a southbound train heading straight at us. Trains don't or can't always stop for animals or people, especially at such close range. We scrambled and managed to get the mother and the black and tan puppy out of harm's way. We were about to catch the white puppy, when the train, with its horn blaring, was coming right at us. We rushed over to the one empty track with the two dogs safely on leashes. The poor little white shepherd puppy couldn't be saved. The train hit the dog, instantly killing it. We picked the dog up in two pieces, cut in half by the wheels of the freight train. My partner was crying. One minute more and we could have saved the beautiful puppy.

One summer night I was working the afternoon shift when I received a call about a tri-coloured shepherd/husky type dog running "at large" on E.C.

Row Expressway. It was around 10 pm, I was driving down the expressway where it crosses Central Avenue, and saw a dog running on the side of the expressway's eastbound lane. Unable to catch the dog, I followed it alongside with all the vans lights flashing. Whenever the dog tried to cross the expressway, I would use the truck and the horn to scare the dog back over to the side of the road. I followed the dog from Central Avenue, which is halfway down the expressway, to Lauzon Road, keeping the dog from getting on the expressway. This is a distance of about 2 miles. I reached Lauzon Road and I thought I had a good chance to catch the dog. I got out of my van and was close to the dog, which was off to the side of the road, but when I got too close, it started running towards the expressway again. Luckily, I had the angle on the dog and ran to cut him off at the pass. While trying to keep this dog away from danger, I hadn't noticed that I was actually on the Expressway lane of traffic myself. When I looked behind me, I saw a car *speeding right at me*. It missed me by half a foot. I said something that resembled *"holy smoke!"*, or *"fudge me!"*. At this point the dog had run back to the side of the road and proceeded towards the eastbound on-ramp. I turned around and proceeded to the ramp. I saw the dog then running from the ramp onto a farmer's field. In spite of my coaxing efforts, the dog went further in the field. At least the dog was out of danger away from the expressway. I left to respond to another call.

The next morning I was dispatched to a call about a dog hit by a car on E.C. Row Expressway on the ramp at Lauzon. It turned out to be the same tri-coloured shepherd/husky that I had tried to help for an hour and a half the night before. The dog didn't make it back to the expressway, but was heading in that direction when it was killed at the ramp.

Probably looking for its master.

Dropping off dogs like this endangers innocent people's lives, often results in the death of the animal, made my job very dangerous, and is, for good reason, against the law.

CHAPTER TWELVE – dogs in my head - every dog has its day

After 32 years at the Humane Society, my ears still ring, 24/7. The medical term for this is *tinnitus*. Mine is tinnitus x 1000. This condition affects a person's sleep, and can drive a person crazy, because, too often it's crazy loud in your head. And it never goes away.

> Tinnitus (TIN-ih-tus) is the perception of noise or ringing in the ears. A common problem,

> tinnitus affects about 1 in 5 people. Tinnitus isn't a condition itself — it's a symptom of an underlying condition, such as age-related hearing loss, ear injury or a circulatory system disorder. The phantom noise may vary in pitch from a low roar to a high squeal, and you may hear it in one or both ears. In some cases, the sound can be so loud it can interfere with your ability to concentrate or hear actual sound. Tinnitus may be present all the time, or it may come and go.
>
> Mayo Clinic website

Hearing protection was not an option for me for all those years because I had to be aware of what was going on around me. Every time I walked through the shelter, each dog cried for my attention with loud, incessant, pointed barking. I couldn't use hearing protection because danger could present itself at any time.

Thousands of dogs came through our shelter during my years there, most of them taken care of by me personally. The vast majority of dogs that came in were either turned in by their owners, strays brought in by the public, or dogs picked up by the Humane Society. There were many reasons why people brought in dogs, some good, some just plain lousy.

Understandable reasons: the owners moved into an apartment where dogs were not allowed, financial reasons, a job loss, a newborn baby, an allergy, etc.

Not so good reasons: the dog got too big, (all German shepherds grow to a big size), it was uncontrollable, (get a trainer), it chewed on the furniture, (buy chew toys especially when the dog is teething). My favourite was: *"We just don't want it anymore."*

(bad attitude) guard dogs

Guard dogs are trained to protect people and property, through violence, if necessary. Many of them die in the process. I always wondered what was done to make so many mean and dangerous. Once a 90 lb. shepherd I was handling bit me on the arm when we were euthanizing it, leaving a big scar on my left forearm. Another time, I was dispatched to pick up a guard dog loose on a city street. The dog ran straight at me, and bit me on the chest.

The owner of a Chinese restaurant located near the shelter on Walker Rd called me up one day and asked if I could help with his guard dog. I knew the gentleman and had been to his restaurant a few times, so I agreed to take a look. The dog was kept in a large dog house in an outside penned area. The owner said the dog wasn't moving very much, wouldn't leave the dog house, wasn't eating much, just seemed sick. I got down and tried to pull the dog out. It took some effort because the dog was so heavy. As I got a little closer to the dog's head, it tried to bite me in the face, and instead mangled my prescription sunglasses. After a few minutes, I tried again and managed to get it out of the dog house, and after a struggle, got it into the van. I brought the dog to the shelter where it was examined by our veterinarian who recommended that the dog be euthanized. After conferring with the owner, the poor guard dog was put down. The restaurant owner later thanked me for taking the dog away. He offered to pay for the sunglasses, but I told him I could always get another pair. He said to come by the restaurant any time I wanted, so I ended up getting great free Chinese food a few times.

CHAPTER THIRTEEN – some more dangerous killer dogs

The Humane Society removed ten pit bull dogs in 1998 from a property out in the county. The dogs and their owners were suspected of being involved in a dog fighting ring and indeed we found tread mills, pry bars and other suspicious materials. The pit bulls were on 10' chains, outside, each one with its own dog house. Of the 10 dogs, by far the most vicious was a white albino adult male. It was my job to remove this dog from the site, and it wasn't an easy task. I had to use the short catchpole and bolt cutters simultaneously, to snap the chain from the dog's collar, all the while avoiding getting seriously bitten by an enraged American pit bull terrier.

Since there would likely be a court case, we had to hold the dogs. Surprisingly, most of them were OK to take care of, except for the white albino, which was completely unpredictable. At times pleasant, other times, not. We kept it in a special run with a chain link roof, because this dog could jump 6 feet high, and with its powerful legs and jaw, jump up to the metal roof, and hang there in midair, dangling by its teeth. The dog was a real Dr. Jekyll and Mr. Hyde.

I took daily care of the dog, brought food and water, and took it outside every day to do its business and get fresh air. Believe it or not, I actually became a friend to this very dangerous dog. Many times I would sit on a small ledge in the doorway with my face next to the dog's head while cleaning discharge from its eyes. For the first few weeks, there were no problems. Then one day as I was letting it out for its run, it jumped up towards my neck, trying to knock me down. I braced for impact, but the pit bull still managed to sink his teeth into the side of my chest, leaving teeth marks. I quickly grabbed the nearby catch pole and put the dog outside. That was a close call.

The dog was being kept alive because it was considered evidence. I wasn't working the following Saturday, so my fellow worker Jackie had to take care of it, and take it outside for its daily. When she opened the run, it leapt up at her and knocked her down. It tried to get at her neck, but she put her arm up to block it, so the dog then caused a lot of damage on her arm, shoulder and leg. Her shouts were heard by Kathy in the office, who alerted Lori. It took Lori and four other Humane Society workers to fend off this vicious dog. Had they not intervened, Jackie could very well have been killed. Our manager Marilyn was notified. After returning from the hospital where Jackie had received 60 stitches and some plastic surgery, Marilyn ordered the dog to be euthanized regardless of the pending court proceedings.

another bad one

One year later I was dispatched to pick up an albino pit bull that was at a house on Janette St. in the city's west end. When a pit bull was involved, a lot of people would freak and call the Humane Society. At-large pit bulls were a priority for us. We quickly got it. I persuaded the dog's owner to sign it over to the Humane Society, and he reluctantly agreed to sign an "Owner Release Form". At the shelter, this dog attacked and badly hurt another worker, Laura, who was caring for it one weekend. Laura and Lori were the only staff in the building that day, which was a holiday, so the office and adoption areas were closed. Lori heard Laura's anguished calls for help from the other side of the building, came running, and saw Laura badly injured. There was blood everywhere. Lori, (who had been involved in the previous pit bull attack) fended the dog off while it was dragging poor Laura around. This pit bull was only eight months old, and had it been a full grown adult, things might have been a lot worse. An ambulance came and Laura was hospitalized with serious injuries. That was it for her career working with dogs.

This can sometimes be a dangerous line of work for anyone, particularly when poorly raised mean pit bulls are involved.

CHAPTER FOURTEEN – dogs, dogs and more dogs; how distracting

In my 32 years working for the Humane Society, I cared for big dogs, little dogs, mean dogs, friendly dogs and killer dogs. Every dog I took care of eventually found out it had to follow my two basic rules:

        Rule #1 – Don't bite me
        Rule #2 – Don't harm other animals
                in the shelter

The humane movement was and is all about people helping animals who cannot speak or fend for themselves and I always tried to help the underdog, and not allow dogs to pick on other dogs. They were all entitled to be protected from harm, including from one another.

We would always try to keep the dogs at the shelter for the shortest period of time possible. In some rare cases, dogs kept at the shelter for too long would start to lose hope and get depressed. In the beginning the dog was happily looking out at the front of the cage hoping for its chance, but after too much time went by it would just give up and stare at the back of the cage or run, defeated. This was always difficult to watch. We would try to lift the dogs' spirits by spending more quality time with them, allowing more time outside, and providing more stimulation, to try to reduce the feeling of desperation a few of these dogs showed.

There were also times when I feared for my own well-being when dealing with the angry or aggressive dogs. In those cases, I tried to avoid making total eye contact, because if a dog sees fear in your eyes, it can get scared, and bite. If I got cornered, or if I had to remove a collar from a vicious dog, a distraction by me or a fellow worker often was my only weapon. I was once handling a vicious shar-pei at the front desk area. I'm sorry to say, but, shar-peis can sometimes be somewhat unfriendly dogs. The dog was in the process of being turned in to us by its owner. I wanted to remove the dog's collar, but I could see it wasn't going to cooperate. I got a co-worker to make a loud noise, and this distracted it just long enough for me to remove its collar. There were many close calls. I've been bit by dogs quite a few times, although luckily nothing major. The two worst bites I received were from German shepherd guard dogs. I never liked guard dogs, because of their nasty personalities, even though I know it was how they were trained that caused this. On the few times I felt the air from a dog's jaw snapping dangerously right next to my head, it was usually from a German shepherd. Even taking them outside was no easy task. Often, they simply did not want to go anywhere. Our policy was to take all dogs outside at least once a day. The mean ones required using the catch pole.

In 1992, I was caring for a male black chow, another breed not always the friendliest. Crippled from a birth defect, its back end paralyzed, this dog couldn't walk, but only prop itself up with its front legs. At first, it would try to bite me every time I carried it outside, but the more attention I gave it, the friendlier it got. I named the dog *Buddy*. I would spend extra time with Buddy, bring it out more than just once a day, and even occasionally give this lovely dog some of my own lunch. We became the best of friends. Because of his poor physical condition and the paralysis, he was really unadoptable. After a few weeks the time came for Buddy to be euthanized. I couldn't do it. I had my partner Blake assist the Vet.

Buddy the Chow

must be a catch

A catch pole is comprised pole with a loop at the end, with a wire running through it. The tautness of the loop is controlled by the operator pulling the wire at the end of the handle. It locks through a mechanism in the hub. They do not harm the animals. The hardest part about using a catch pole is with a dangerous or vicious dog on the loose. Accuracy and precision are required, more so with an angry canine. The operator's safety and that of the public is threatened by these dogs.

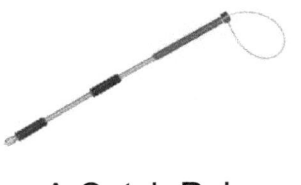

A Catch Pole
(ketch-all.com)

It's safe to say that many, many dogs came into our shelter angry at the world, and were successfully transformed back into being Man's Best Friend. The Humane Society took good care of all kinds of dogs. Some were abused, some neglected, and some just scared. All of this damage was caused by humans. I tried to undo everything that was done to them, to treat the dogs well in order to gain their trust. A few dogs were unreachable and could not be rehabilitated. Those dogs usually had suffered physical and emotional abuse at the hands of bad people, and in those cases, with no recourse, had to be put down.

CHAPTER FIFTEEN – cops – who ya gonna call?

The Windsor/Essex County Humane Society had excellent working relations with all the Police Forces throughout Windsor and Essex County.

In the years before 1999, when the Windsor Humane Society became an affiliate of the OSPCA, we relied on the police to sign our Animal Removal and Animal in Distress Orders. The police were there when we needed protection and we assisted them in animal matters where our expertise was required.

I received a call from the Windsor Police one night to remove a dog from a Jeep that was holding up traffic at the Windsor Tunnel entrance. When I got there, the owner had been arrested, and the traffic was backed up for a few blocks. The officer told me we needed to get the situation cleared up quickly. One problem. Inside the car was a large and unfriendly doberman-pinscher, still guarding its master's property. Whenever I opened the door, it jumped at me. Slowly but surely I placed my leash in position and just slightly opened the door. His head went into the leash and I pulled him out. I placed the doberman in my van, the car was moved, and the flow of traffic resumed.

One afternoon in 1985, I received a call about a dog hit by a car and still stuck underneath it on Riverside Dr. It was rush hour, and traffic was getting seriously backed up behind the car. The driver didn't want to move the car, because he thought it might further injure the freaked out dog. At the time I got the call, I was at the corner of Erie and McDougall Street, stuck at a red light. It being an emergency, I decided to go through the red light. The next thing I knew, I was pulled over by an angry cop and given a ticket for running a red light. When I arrived at the stuck dog situation, the police were there, holding up the increasingly backed up traffic. The officer at the scene snapped,

"Where have you been? We've been waiting for you. Look at the traffic that's backed up." I said, *"Hey, I got a ticket on my way here. That's what held me up."*

He just shook his head as I proceeded to crawl under the car and to pull the dog out. It was difficult because it was a 90 lb. German shepherd wedged under the car pretty good. Eventually I got the very scared dog out, and brought it to a veterinarian for treatment. It was ok.

The next day I got a call from the Staff Sargent at Windsor Police Headquarters. He happened to be an officer that I knew well. He told me to come down to the station and bring the ticket that I got the day before. When I got there the Sargent said *"Give me that",* and ripped the ticket up.

dead men tell no tails

Occasionally when people passed away, the police would call us up for assistance in removing any animals owned by the deceased.

I attended 5 or 6 of these calls. Sometimes the person had just died, other times they had been dead for quite a while. In the latter case, there would be a very strong odour of death in the house or apartment. The attending police officer sometimes asked if I wanted to wait for the coroner. Usually I just would go in, and would see the deceased person just lying there, then get the pet I didn't liked doing that part of the job, but it had to be done. After the deceased person's animal was brought to the shelter, a hold was put on the I.D. card. We then tried to locate any next of kin. If none was found, the pet was put up for adoption.

a paws in the traffic – revenge is sweet

I observed a man driving a pickup truck with a dog in the cargo area. This was on Tecumseh Road, one of the busiest streets in Windsor. I considered this a very dangerous situation for the dog on a busy street. The dog should have been in the cab area of the truck, or in a travel cage. You all know this.

At a red light at Pillete Road, I rolled the passenger side window down and politely told the man the dog was in danger and should be inside the cab of the truck. He immediately looked over and told me to *"F--- Off"*, and gave me a raised middle finger. *My goodness*, I quietly muttered to myself. When the light turned green, he continued down the road, with the black lab still in the back.

I had two choices – either I forget about it, or I call our friends at the Windsor Police Department. I radioed into my dispatch, gave my location and the direction I was heading, and told them a dog was in danger. In a matter of 10 minutes, I saw the police car approaching not too far behind us. Animals in distress always got prompt attention from the Windsor Police.

The man was pulled over by one of Windsor's finest. I pulled over, got out of my van and told the officer that the guy had to, by law, put his dog in the cab. The truck owner quickly put the dog in the cab. The officer asked me if there was anything else.

Remembering the drivers' rudeness, I said there was. Acting on a hunch, I went over to the pickup truck driver and asked him if he had a current dog licence. A bit sheepishly, he admitted he did not have one for his now safe lab. I happily gave him a ticket.

friends indeed; - everybody plays a fool

One night near the end of my shift, I was on my way to drop the Humane Society truck off at my co-worker Keith's home. Since he was on call overnight, I needed to get the van to him by midnight.

I was on Howard Avenue in the northbound lane. There is a major railway level crossing at Memorial Drive, one of the major railway crossings in the city. The gates were down on both sides, and the lights were flashing. I looked and saw no train coming from either direction. Impatient, I decided to go around the gate, and proceeded to turn right down Memorial Drive.

Unfortunately for me, there was a police car in the southbound lane on the other side of the train gates. The testy officer pulled me over, and yelled at me *"What the hell is wrong with you?"*, and went on to say that what I did would result in a big fine and points on my driver's license. He went to the police car, talked on his radio, let me sit there for a few minutes and then got out of the squad car and came back to the van. I was expecting the worst. He looked at me, pointing his finger and said *"You know better than that. Now get out of here!"*

Another time, I was on Provincial Road where the speed limit was 60 kph. I happened to be travelling closer to 80 kph. I noticed a police car with lights a-flashing. I was pulled over. He told me *"You Humane Society guys use this road like a speedway"*. He called dispatch and ran my information. I had made quite a few friends on the Windsor Police force during my years at the Humane Society, so when my information went out over the police radio airwaves, a very good friend of mine on the force heard everything. He came 15 minutes out of his way and talked to the officer who was in the midst of writing my ticket. After a short conversation, the officer folded his ticket book, then turned to me and said *"You're lucky this guy is your friend. Now you owe him a dinner."* I thanked them both and was on my way.

And I gladly bought him dinner.

CHAPTER SIXTEEN – circus inspections

Circuses today are very different than they were 25, or even 5 years ago. An increasing number of them don't use animals at all as part of their shows anymore. As a result of very intense lobbying by animal activist groups and Humane Societies, elephants, seals, bears, monkeys, lions, tigers, and even dogs are being used far less under the Big Top. Barnum & Bailey, in business since 1871, packed it in for good in 2017.

Circus inspections were part of my job as an officer working for the Windsor/Essex County Humane Society. I was required to inspect the transportation and living conditions of the animals. Sometimes we would be invited by the circus owner, other times we would show up on our own.

I was never an expert on exotic animals. Most of my work was done with dogs, cats, and wildlife. Nevertheless, when inspecting a circus, I checked the animals' general health and appearance, their food, water and housing, looking for signs of neglect or abuse. I examined their transport vehicles, the specialized trailers, stake trucks, and big transport trailers circuses used. I was not privy to their training techniques, or how the trainers got the animals to perform for their shows.

At one of the first circuses I inspected, I noticed the elephants swaying back and forth. Even I knew this behavior was caused by boredom, frustration and a lack of stimulus. I asked the attendant why these elephants were doing this. He told me, *"That's what they do when they're happy"*. I disagreed, chuckling to myself, *sotto voce*. He immediately got defensive, and said he knew a lot more about elephants than I did. That may have been true, but I remained unconvinced. Noting that there was nothing physically wrong with these elephants, no outward injuries and disabilities (limping), no apparent malnutrition or dehydration, there was really nothing I could do.

In the summer of 2003 the Humane Society got a call from Ian Garden of the famous Garden Bros. Circus, a circus that had been in business in North America for a century. Mr. Garden invited us to inspect his circus. When I arrived at the Windsor Arena, there were about a dozen people protesting at the front box office door, one carrying a sign that read:

ANIMALS SUFFER IN THE CIRCUS

I went to Garden's personal trailer. He struck me as a nice enough guy. He took me around his circus to each of the areas were the animals and trainers were working. I spoke to John Campolongo, who showed me the circus tigers. He said he was their actual owner and trainer.

There were four adult Bengal tigers, each in their individual cages. He told me that he cared very much for his cats, that he was second generation at this, and that he was very proud of them. The tigers appeared healthy to me, as I watched him feeding them. The cages were clean, so were the transport cages. On this particular inspection, *Life Network* happened to be filming their series called *Circus*. Parts of my inspection actually appeared on the exposé. I'm a star.

Panthear tigris tigris, or Bengal tiger
(tigers-world.com)

Next, I met with Michael Hackenberger, the trainer for the famous Angus the Elephant. Angus, who was 24 years old at the time, actually had made his home for 20 years at the Bowmanville Zoo, located east of Toronto, when he wasn't on the road with the Garden Bros. Circus. Angus was the world's largest elephant then held in captivity. He once swam with whales in the St Lawrence River. He died at the age of 27, in 2006, just before being repatriated to an elephant game reserve in South Africa. Hackenberger was heartbroken at the loss of his dear friend, Angus the Elephant. So were many others.

On my inspection that day, Hackenberger was in the process of watering down the 7 ton elephant. The elephant seemed healthy to me, and was happily chewing on a tree branch when I got there. I inspected the housing and the transport vehicle. Everything seemed to be in order.

Michael Hackenberger with Angus
(Photo Rachel Mendleson / Toronto Star)

I looked over some performing ducks, their cages and transport vehicle. The cages were clean and they had adequate food and fresh water. The dogs appeared healthy, had plenty of food, fresh water, and clean shelter. All the transport vehicles checked out. I got to observe Mr. Garden's prized Arabian horse. It also appeared healthy.

It was only later that I learned that Garden Bros. Circus had been in a lot of hot water, after my visit, over the way they had been treating their animals in other locales. At the risk of offending my good friends who are animal activists, I have to say that my inspection in the summer of 2003 indicated that everything appeared to be OK. People, including animal activists, have to understand that in most inspections we could only see what was in front of us. We didn't get behind the scenes looks, or observe any training exercises. It was a snapshot visual inspection, no more, no less. And what I saw, in my opinion, passed inspection.

CHAPTER SEVENTEEN – life at the shelter – esprit de corps des chats et des chiens

The Shelter was the focal point for animal welfare in the City and County. The current building was constructed in 1970. Since then, there have been a number of additions and enhancements. The spay and neuter clinic was added in 2011. Later came a dog park, with indoor and outdoor runs.

It could be a roller coaster of happiness and heartaches for us. We saw the worst in a lot of people, but those who supported the Humane

Society were generous to a fault. Donors came in from all walks of life, from factory workers to neurosurgeons to professors to business people. Yes, even some lawyers.

We used laughter to get through the heartaches. We were a family and we all depended upon each other. One afternoon when I was on the road, I booked off for lunch at noon to be back at 1:00, but I accidently fell asleep. It was almost 3 pm when I woke up. The manager was asking where I was. Jeanne, covering for me, said I had gone into a field after a stray dog. The boss noted that was two hours ago. Jeanne said *"It was a big field"*.

The goal was to get good homes for each and every animal, if that was possible. It was such a lovely sight watching people bond with a new pet, knowing that these animals were going to good homes for many happy years.

Melanie was (and still is at the time of writing) the Executive Director of the Windsor/Essex County Humane Society. She believed in putting the animals first. She was always coming up with innovative and imaginative ways to increase adoption rates. She held a 2 for 1 sale for cats, had a sale on black cats on Halloween, promoted cats and dogs for sale at Christmas. She held Adopt-a-thons and Walk-a-thons.

For many years the employee in charge of the adoption area was Aline, who was known as "Ma" to all of us. She had worked at the Humane Society longer than anybody. Ma called us her "*lost children*". I had a down filled jacket that I had gotten dirty crawling under a porch deck, scrounging for an injured cat. Ma saw my coat and took it away to clean it. She didn't see the DRY CLEAN ONLY tag, so it came back to me with all the filling clumped up on the back. I looked like the Hunchback of Notre Dame. Everyone laughed. We still laugh about it. Maybe, you had to be there, but this was one of many examples of the *camaraderie* at the shelter.

When people had a missing pet, the Humane Society usually was the first place they looked. A lot of these distraught people would tell me where they lived and me knowing most of the neighborhoods in the city like the back of my hand, I would give them ideas where to search. Often, this helped reunite owners and their pets. I got a lot of calls from people thanking me for this. A good feeling all around.

We saw anxious cat and dog owners who would visit the shelter every day for months on end, hoping to be re-united with their pets. In 1999, the Humane Society introduced cat tags with an ID number similar to the dog tags already available. We made the *Windsor Star* about this. This caused a big surge in people coming for these tags, which were eventually replaced by the superior micro-chips.

My friend Gail, a volunteer at the Shelter, initiated a program we called *"Animal Return",* which I helped on. Gail would search the internet, newspapers, signs posted on telephone poles, grocery store message boards and other community notice boards. She would then check the information against all the animals in the intake area. Many people were re-united with their pets because of Gail's valiant efforts to help people.

I had a trick I used in situations with angry people who were picking up their dog demanding to know who brought the dog in. If it was me, I would say *"Fritz did"*. If they asked *"Where's Fritz?"* I would say *"He's not here right now"*. This worked many times, and became a trick used by all of us.

Fritz with Fritz
(Photo by Ted Rhodes, Windsor Star)

One day an irate gentleman was berating the receptionist at the desk, demanding to know just where "*Fritz*" was. Steve, my buddy, getting tired of listening to this guy, stood up and said *"I'm Fritz, got a problem with that?"* The guy cooled down.

We witnessed the sorrow of people bringing in their pets to have them euthanized. We dealt with animals getting dropped off after hours, often in boxes or make-shift containers. Sometimes they would escape. For many years, I was the last person to leave the shelter at the end of the day and normally I would lock up and exit the parking lot to go home. I would notice people at the front door ringing the buzzer with boxes of kittens, stray dogs, cats or injured wildlife. On my own time, I would go back into the building, go to the front, and book the animal(s) in. This happened to me alone at least 50 times.

christmas at the shelter

The huge outpouring of generosity towards the animals and staff at Christmas was something to behold. It warmed our hearts. Windsor and county people would bring in countless donations for the animals at the shelter. The gifts included food and kibble, treats, rawhides, litter, cat beds, dog beds, and sleighs - and boatloads full of cat and dog toys. Canada Border Services, and other groups and individuals would send boxes of stuff. The animals were not going to be forgotten at Christmas. I even think they knew what was going on. The staff were not forgotten either. Candies, chocolates, pastries, snacks of all kinds flooded the shelter. For a few years, Anna from Canada Customs provided the whole shelter staff with a catered lunch.

Santa at the shelter
(Photo Humane Society Staff)

shelter stand-off

Anyone asking about a lost pet was taken through the whole pound. If the pet was there, staff would take the ID card off the cage and bring it to the front office for processing. The relieved owner would come with us to the front desk for some paperwork, but the pet had to stay in the penalty box until the paperwork was complete. There would be a fee to claim the animal. A dog would cost more than a cat because of the additional running-at-large fine, and sometimes a license fee. Remember, cats can roam free, unlicensed.

One day in 1992, a man in his 30's came in looking for his black lab. I took him through to check on the dogs in the pound area and we came to his dog, which was clearly very happy to see its master, tail going a mile a minute. As per protocol, I took the ID card and turned towards the door of the dog room to proceed to the office for the necessary processing.

```
Pound Record Card
                                              No 40856
Date in _____
                        Time
                             a.m.             On Arrival
Owned ❏    Truck _____ pm                   Sick     ❏
                             a.m.
Stray  ❏   Pound _____ pm                   injured  ❏
                                              Dead     ❏
Location _____
Breed of Animal _____
  Dog  ❏            M ❏              Spayed   ❏
  Cat  ❏            F ❏              Neutered ❏
  Other ❏                            Declawed ❏
Windsor License # _____  Misc. # _____
                        Description
Est. Age _____  Est. Weight _____
                        Mark or
Colour _____      Collar
Owner: _____ Phone: _____
Address: _____

 Sold ❏        Claimed ❏         Destroyed ❏
 Other ❏ _____

Pound Keeper's Signature _____ Date Out _____
Feed:    Dry     Canned    Puppy Chow    Kitten Chow
Vaccines Given: _____

Treatments Given: _____

Veterinarian's Comments: _____

General Comments: _____
```

The man opened the cage and took his dog out. I explained that the card had to be processed before the dog could be released. He stated, *"It's my dog, I don't care. I'm taking it"*, put his own collar on the dog and proceeded to walk out. I in turn put my own leash on the dog and stopped the guy from moving any further. There we were in the middle of the hallway, the man trying to take the dog out, and me holding the dog back. It was a stand-off, neither of us budging. Five minutes went by. Then ten. I expected the guy any second to punch me out. Someone on the front desk called the police, and a Windsor police officer was soon on the scene. When the guy saw the cop, he paid his fee and the shelter standoff ended, with no casualties. The dog was not hurt at any time.

CHAPTER EIGHTEEN – mascots

Our adopted pets, humane society *mascots*, had the run of the place, including the office area. Over the years we were lucky to have so many. They were our ambassadors of goodwill.

Sam – conflict resolution

A tan coloured shepherd retriever mix, Sam was our policeman. At 65 pounds, he had a commanding but subtle presence. He hung out in the front office most of the time, away from the other animals. Sam always had a friendly greeting for us and anybody else who came to the shelter. That is, unless someone came in angry or animated, complaining, cursing, causing a ruckus, irate about a claiming fee, or a stray dog in the neighbourhood. Sam would immediately, without growling or biting, go directly and sit right next to the perpetrator, and glare at him. He was a very effective tension de-fuser. This always got a laugh out of us.

pickles

Pickles was a tri-coloured female Spaniel/Border Collie who came to us from the streets of downtown Windsor. She had become a celebrity with everybody in the downtown area, many of whom provided food for her, including restaurant owners and staff. She was a totally free spirit. There were stories in the newspaper and on local television news about her many exploits. She was the subject of a terrific kid's book, "*PICKLES, Street Dog of Windsor",* 1985 Black Press, Windsor, Amazon.ca) written by author Sean O Huigin, with lovely illustrations by Phil McLeod. During her time at the shelter, people would come to visit her, or call asking how she was doing. She was a real celebrity. It was a very sad day at the shelter on

Tuesday October 29th, 1985 when our beloved *Pickles the Wonder Dog* died.

Pickles – the Wonder Dog

peaches

Then we had Peaches, a tan and white female spaniel/collie mix. In the winter of 1984 we received a call about a dog stranded on Peche Island. Peche Island is in the Detroit River, right where it meets Lake St Clair.

Peche Island from the Windsor side
(Photo windsorpubliclibrary.com)

Another Windsor landmark, Peche Island is a 35 hectare (86 acre) marsh-like island situated where the Detroit River meets Lake St Clair. Chief Pontiac used it as a fishing village. Successive owners have included Hiram Walker (who had a 40 room mansion built there, along with a marina and a golf course), some hucksters in the 1960s with plans for a ski hill and an amusement park with residential development, the Canadian government, the Province of Ontario, and now the City of Windsor, which runs a shuttle to and from the island in the summer, giving everybody a chance to enjoy the wildlife and the beaches. The island is host to a wide variety of waterfowl (common merganser, swans, mallards), birds

(Peregrine falcons, bald eagles), and fishing including, bass, perch, pickerel, carp and the occasional muskie (muskelonge). (partial source - Wikipedia)

It was very cold that year, and the Detroit River had iced up around the island and along the Windsor side of the river. Somehow Peaches had ended up on an ice flow while roaming the shoreline area, and floated on it over to Peche Island. When the ice flow broke up, she ended up stranded on the empty island. Someone had spotted her and called us, and with the help of a local canoe club, she was rescued and brought to the shelter. We named her *Peaches*, after the Island, which had been, and still sometimes is, colloquially called by some older locals, *Peach* Island. Peaches was never claimed, and she became a mascot for us. She was a sweet, quiet dog, and got along quite well with her fellow mascots, Sam and Pickles. Great dogs.

murphy

Murphy was a black and tan male lab/shepherd, picked up as a stray on a Windsor city street. This was after Pickles and Peaches had gone, and Sam was in his last days. Murphy was warm and super friendly. Everyone at the shelter fell in love with our Murphy. He was not claimed and we all decided unanimously that he would be a great mascot.

Things went well for his first month there, but then suddenly one day, out of character, he snuck out the front door. Jeanne, our receptionist rushed out after him. Murphy ran straight towards the busy road, and in a matter of seconds, he was struck down and killed by a car.

I can still see Jeanne carrying Murphy back to the shelter crying her eyes out.

whitney and the rat

In the mid 90's a white border collie came in as a stray. We named her *Whitney* and decided to keep her as a mascot. Like most border collies, she was bright, intelligent, alert, and friendly. We afforded her the privilege of sleeping in her own dog bed in the office. One day Whitney slipped out the front door of the building. I went right out after her. After a frantic search, I finally saw her at the side of the building just sitting still, staring at a rat she had trapped in the corner. The terrified rat was not moving. Remembering one should never corner a rat (one jumped at my face in an alley once), I called her away. She somewhat reluctantly complied. Yet another wonder dog as a mascot for us.

Emmy, our Humane Education teacher, fell in love with Whitney, and took her home (no further discussion was necessary). She took Whitney to some of the classes. All the kids loved her.

and also some hilarious cat mascots

j.r.

We got our first cat mascot in 1983, a cat we called *J.R.* He was named after the evil character in the TV series *Dallas.* He wasn't the friendliest cat, but he loved being at the shelter with all its activity. J.R. seemed at all times to understand everything that was going on. A brown and white tabby male, he stayed with us for about 5 years.

fox, and sweet melissa

These two cat mascots came in together, turned in by a family who could no longer care of them. Fox, a grey and white female tabby, and Melissa, a brown female tabby, were welcome members of our family at the Humane Society. Melissa was shy and reserved, and pretty well kept to herself. Fox was a people cat. She spent most of her time at the front desk inter-acting with everyone. As soon as anyone made eye contact with her, she would come over, start a conversation, and enjoy the attention.

the artful dupester

Then along came *Dupester*, a large, grey male who prowled around the shelter at all hours. Originally called *Horrible Harry* by Marilyn our manager, we changed his name to Dupester because whenever someone tried to pick him up, he would try to dupe them. He hated being picked up by anyone. Norm was the only exception.

One morning the Dupester wandered into the back of the building where euthanasia was being done. He got too close to a husky that had been tranquilized and was sitting there. The dog reached over and bit the Dupester, holding him down, trying to do more damage. I was walking by and pulled our mascot away from the clutches of the mean husky. He ended up with quite a few stitches, but after about a month, the Dupester was back to his old self.

dennis the menace and tommy – most loved mascots of all

Dennis and Tommy were both orange male tabbies, brought to the shelter in 1995, by a truly sad owner who could no longer care for them. Dennis the Menace loved inter-acting with everyone, and spent most of his time at the front desk, stepping on keyboards, hanging up phones and generally getting into everything. He was often seen chewing on the corner of donated food bags sampling their contents, or knocking down open bags to feast. He didn't get his knick-name for nothing.

""Windsor/Essex County Humane Society mascot cat Dennis bites Essex MP Jeff Watson on the chin in January 2010. Dennis died August 26, 2011 at the age of 19".
(Photo by Nick Brancaccio, story The Windsor Star)

Tommy on the other hand was very shy and reserved. A more loyal friend you couldn't find anywhere. Tommy, our mascot was loved by everybody, staff and visitors alike. Once, I had to spend a whole night at the shelter doing security, and Tommy never once left my side.

Mascot Tommy
(Photo by Humane Society staff)

Every day at precisely 8am, when I started work, Tommy would come and spend quality time with me, We became the best of friends. Sadly, one Saturday morning when I was home sick, a pit bull had got loose and quickly came to the inner office where Tommy was waiting for me. Tommy was killed. When they called me, I cried over the loss of my good friend, Tommy. Still bothers me.

Dennis carried on without Tommy. Eventually, glaucoma claimed his right eye but this didn't stop him from being the Dennis the Menace we all loved. He was famous for his friendly bites on your chin, and his meow that sounded more like he was saying "COW". When Dennis was dying, I held him in my arms. He gave me one last love bite on my chin before he drew his last breath. What a great cat he was.

eddie

We adopted a third cat mascot, "*Eddie*", a black and white male cat who came to the Humane Society from a farm. Whenever animals were brought in to the reception area he acted as the greeting committee. Eddie would lick kittens, rabbits and puppies, letting them know they were welcome.

freddie

Our last mascot in my time there was also a black and white male long haired cat. He looked a little like Eddie so we called him Freddie. He was very friendly and was a great addition to the shelter family. Another great cat, smart and kind.

Rizzo

For 5 years my work week consisted of 4 night shifts and 1 day shift on Saturday. I would often be seen driving the streets of Windsor with Rizzo, my trusty sidekick, in the passenger seat of the Humane Society van. It was too dangerous to have Rizzo with me at night, but every Saturday, she would travel with me.

My Saturday shift started at 9:00 am and like clockwork at 8:30, Rizzo would be waiting anxiously by the door ready to go with me to work. She knew it was my Saturday shift. She loved the adventure of driving the streets of Windsor in the Humane Society van, always on the lookout for her animal friends.

Rizzo was my best friend for 17 years. I still miss her.

Rizzo
1977 – 1994

CHAPTER NINETEEN – short notes and miscellany

gordie howe and the pesky widdo wabbit

Gordie Howe, "Mr. Hockey", was in Windsor, fund raising for the Humane Society. Howe devoted much of his time helping charities and organizations, with fund-raising and special events, including ours.

That's right, when I was there, the Great Gordie Howe visited our shelter on Provincial Road in Windsor. John, our manager took Gordie on a tour of the shelter. I was working in the Wildlife Room with rabbits, guinea pigs, gerbils and a few birds. When they came to my area, John introduced me to Gordie Howe. That was a thrill, I must say.

I was in the process of cleaning a cage that held a very mean white and brown adult rabbit that had been turned in by some people who were afraid of it. Howe was watching what I was doing. I explained that the rabbit wasn't very friendly and didn't like people coming near it. Gordie immediately stuck his hand in the cage and, surprisingly, the rabbit just sat there and didn't try to bite him. The rabbit must have known with whom it was dealing. Off the ice Gordie Howe was an incredibly selfless man who believed in giving, rather than taking. He was always willing to sign an autograph for young and old alike, or help a worthwhile cause. It was his way of giving back.

He was a bit different on the ice.

On May 14, 2015 the new bridge between Windsor and Detroit (Canada & the USA) was named The Gordie Howe International Bridge. Howe, 87 and in failing health could not attend the ceremony. In his father's last days, his son, Dr. Murray Howe, brought Gordie to the banks of the Detroit River where the bridge was to be constructed and Mr.

Hockey saw for himself where one of his legacies would be.

Artist's rendering of The Gordie Howe International Bridge

(Photo Courtesy of the Windsor-Detroit Bridge Authority / Windsor Star)

sally the liberator

Sally, bless her soul, was an animal lover who respected all the creatures on this earth. She was the sister of a very close friend of mine.

She called me about a beagle owned by her next door neighbour. She said the owner paid very little attention to the dog that sat, day after day in a penned area, its only company when the owner showed up to top-up feed and water, and clean the pen. After that, the dog spent the rest of its time in solitary confinement.

So, I attended one afternoon and spoke to the owner. The man took me to the pen to check on the dog. The pen was a good size with plenty of room for a 38 lb. beagle. There was plenty of clean water. The dog was friendly and healthy looking. I left having found no real problems, other than loneliness. I told Sally that as far as I knew, there was no real law requiring an owner to pay attention to a dog as long as necessities of life were provided.

One day at 6:30 am, while it was still dark and I was still at home, Sally called. She said *"I've got the dog, you know, the beagle next door."* I told her *"Sally, you just can't steal someone's dog."* She stated *"I liberated it. I didn't steal it. They probably won't even care. That dog was in prison."*

She was a few blocks away from the Humane Society, at a pay phone. I went to see her. She happily turned the dog over to me. I brought the dog into the shelter and booked the beagle in, and provided it with food, water, and a blanket.

A week went by, and no one came around to the shelter looking for the liberated beagle. After two weeks the friendly beagle was in our adoption area and available to adopt. In a matter of days a family fell in love with the dog, and the very happy beagle was in a new home. I called Sally and told her about the dog's good fortune. She was delighted. I asked her if her neighbour seemed bothered about the dog being missing. She said it didn't seem to matter to him. The last time I saw Sally before she passed away, I reminded her of her daring act of liberation.

sammy's story - a second chance - a vet writes from a dog's perspective

This story was written by my good friend Dr. Jim Sweetman from Downtown Veterinary Hospital, Windsor.

He wrote the piece after I brought in a small terrier mix to his hospital for examination and treatment. He wrote the story under the pseudonym of *A. Gator*, the name of his Airedale terrier.

Dr. Jim and I worked together numerous times and he taught me a lot about animal health.

This was in our bulletin:

I never knew my father. My mother was not spayed and was roaming the street when they met. Sixty-three days later, ten of us were crying in the cold garage at the back of someone's house.

Life was fun exploring the old shed, cuddling with my mom and chewing the arms and legs of my mates. When I was in my 5th week, I met a young person who fell in love with me. He was fascinated with my soft white hair and my generous kisses. One afternoon, when he was visiting, I found myself tucked up under his arm. We left the safety of my backyard, crossed several busy streets and finally ended up in his backyard.

At six o'clock, his parents came home. There were not pleased that I was visiting. I suggested that they take me back but somehow I could not communicate this to them. It got pretty cold that night and I started crying. Finally, a big human took me into the house. It was nice and warm. He put me on some funny artificial grass which I now know is called a rug. After they fed me human food, I urinated on the grass. Halfway through my pee, a big human started yelling at me. My mom taught me to urinate on grass! Where is my mom?

After that, things happened very fast. A large hard shoe kicked me across the room. I hit the corner of the space heater and heard a snap. Someone grabbed my scruff and threw me out the door. I limped under the evergreen bush and hid until morning.

The little human came out and fed me some crackers but I really was not hungry. My leg, right by the knee, was aching and was all swollen. I lived in that picky shrub for 3 days, surviving on crackers, a little cheese and milk. I was cold, hungry, sore and missed my mother.

A man in blue walked up to me. He had those big, dark shoes on! Was he going to kick me too? He got down on his hands and knees and gently lifted me into his strong arms. He turned to the big, mean human and said: "I'll take care of this little fellow". He took me in a yellow truck (I sat on his lap – you are not supposed to do that) to a veterinarian. I heard him talk to a lady in white. "This is a real nice little fellow that deserves a chance. Let's talk to the vet and see if we can fix his leg?" I gave him a little kiss.

I stayed in the hospital for 3 days before they put me to sleep. When I woke up, I had a big blue cast on my sore leg. I lived in the hospital for another week. During this time, I learned that injured stray cats and dogs are put to sleep permanently. Why was I given a second chance? I can only think the Humane Society Officer, Mr. Carlos.

I have a steel pin in my leg. It comes out just behind my knee cap. The vet says it has to come out in 5 or weeks. There will be no charges for this. I need a home, love and a name. Ask the receptionist about my medical file. Please give me a second chance!

A. Gator

The happy ending to the above – Sammy got adopted very soon after.

Sammy

student co-op program

The Windsor/Essex County Humane Society had good working relations with area high schools. The Humane Society Student Co-Op Program was very successful. Students would volunteer at the Humane Society for a set number of hours which would count towards their high school credit. The program worked out well for both sides. On the one hand, we got some extra help, and on the other hand, the students, most of them animal lovers, got to work with dogs, cats and other animals and get credit.

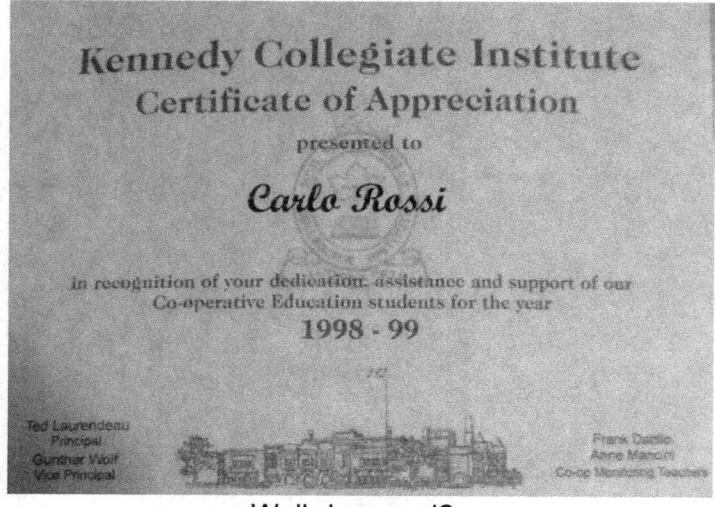

Well-deserved?

ADDENDUM - ANTI-CRUELTY LAWS

CANADA - CRIMINAL CODE OF CANADA

Section 445.1(1)

Every one commits an offence:

1. who willfully causes or, being the owner, wilfully permits to be caused unnecessary pain, suffering or injury to an animal or a bird; in any manner encourages, aids or assists at the fighting or baiting of animals or birds;
2. willfully, without reasonable excuse, administers a poisonous or an injurious drug or substance to a domestic animal or bird or an animal or a bird wild by nature that is kept in captivity or, being the owner of such an animal or a bird wilfully permits a poisonous or an injurious drug or substance to be administered to it;
3. promotes, arranges, conducts, assists in, receives money for or takes part in any meeting, competition, exhibition, pastime, practice, display or event at or in the course of which captive birds are liberated by hand,

trap, contrivance or any other means for the purpose of being shot when they are liberated;
4. Being the owner, occupier or person in charge of any premises, permits the premises or any part thereof to be used for a purpose mentioned in paragraph (d).

Punishment

Every one who commits an offence under subsection (1) is guilty of;
- a) an indictable offence and liable to imprisonment for a term of not more than five years; or
- b) an offence punishable on summary conviction and liable to a fine not exceeding ten thousand dollars or to imprisonment for a term of not more than eighteen months or to both.

ONTARIO – Ontario Society for the Prevention of Cruelty to Animals Act

3. The object of the Society is to facilitate and provide for the prevention of cruelty to animals and their protection and relief therefrom.

10 (5) No person shall hinder, obstruct or interfere with an inspector or an agent of the Society in the performance of his or her duties under this Act.

11.1 (1) Every person who owns or has custody or care of an animal shall comply with the prescribed standards of care, and the prescribed administrative requirements, with respect to every animal that the person owns or has custody or care of.

11.2 (1) No person shall cause an animal to be in distress

11.2 (2) No owner or custodian of an animal shall permit the animal to be in distress.

11.2 (3) No person shall train an animal to fight with another animal or permit an animal that the person owns or has custody or care of to fight another animal.

11.2 (4) No person shall own or have possession of equipment or structures that are used in animal fights or in training animals to fight

11.2 (5) No person shall harm or cause harm to a dog, horse or other animal that works with peace officers in the execution of their duties, whether or not the animal is working at the time of the harm.

11.3 Every veterinarian who has reasonable grounds to believe that an animal has been or is being abused or neglected shall report his or her belief to an inspector or an agent of the Society.

CITY OF WINDSOR
BY-LAW

Any person who owns an animal shall:

1. treat it in a humane manner;

2. keep it so that,
   a) offensive odours and the transfer of disease are minimized,
   b) a female animal in heat does not attract other animals,
   c) there is a suitable exercise area for each animal,
   d) the animal cannot readily escape;
3. provide the necessary food, water, housing and attention as required to keep the animal in good health and free from harm
4. remove forthwith any excrement of the said animal and dispose of it in a sanitary manner.
   a) any person who owns an animal that is customarily kept outside shall at all times:

(i) provide it with protection from the elements including harmful temperatures;

(ii) provide a structurally sound, weatherproof, insulated shelter, of a size and design having regard for the animal's weight of type of coat;

(iii) provide an enclosure which has sufficient space to allow the animal the ability to turn around freely and to easily sit, stand and lie in a fully extended position.

No person shall keep an animal tethered on a rope, chain, cord or similar restraining device unless:

(i) The tether is of appropriate length for the species tethered; i.e. 5 times the length of the dog from the nose to the base of the tail except for small dogs – (should be a minimum of 3 metres);

(ii) the animal has unrestricted movement within the range of such tether;
(iii) the animal is not tethered for longer than 4 hours per day;
(iv) the animal has access to water, and shelter while tethered; and
(v) The animal cannot injure itself as a result of the tethering. (Added B/L)

b) No person shall keep, or cause to be kept, at or in any premises,
   i. more than two of each kind of animal
   ii. any domestic fowl, horses, donkeys, mules, cattle, goats, swine, mink, fox, sheep, ferrets, or chinchillas;
   iii. more than eighty (80) pigeons
   iv. more than four cats
   v. more than three dogs
   vi. more than 2 caged birds may be kept

c) No person shall keep or cause to be kept:
   i. any snake, reptile, insect or spider not otherwise prohibited by this

by-law unless they are housed in an escape-proof enclosure;

ii any guinea pigs, white rats or pigeons unless they are housed in a suitable enclosure.

8. No person who owns any animal shall permit such animal to be at large within the City of Windsor.

12. Every person who contravenes any of the provisions of this by-law (Chapter) is guilty of an offence and shall, upon conviction thereof, forfeit and pay a penalty of not more than Five Thousand Dollars ($5,000)

The Author

Carlo Rossi was born in Nottingham, England in 1951, and came to Windsor, Ontario in 1955. Raised in south Windsor, since 1967 he has played his Ludwig drums for many musical groups in the area. In 1973, he started working at Ford Motor Company, but after almost 5 years, the music bug struck again, and since the shiftwork did not allow him to play regularly, he quit and resumed the band business full-time. At 31 years old and with an uncertain future, he got a job with the Windsor/Essex County Humane Society, where he spent the next 32 years of his life as an officer SPCA agent and animal care worker. Over the years, he helped, rescued, and cared for thousands and thousands of animals. Over 800 people sent him warm congratulations on his retirement on the Humane Society Facebook page.

The Editor

Tim Williamson was born in Welland, Ontario in 1953, and moved with his family to Windsor in 1955. His father taught history for many years at downtown Patterson Collegiate. Tim attended Herman Collegiate through grade 12, and Belle River District High School and graduated from grade 13 in 1971. He studied history and political science at the University of Windsor for 2 years, and then at age 19, he was accepted into law school at Windsor. During his university days, he earned money for tuition by working at the Windsor Chrysler Assembly plant, part-time shoe and light bulb sales, and playing in a band. Upon graduation with a Bachelor of Laws degree in 1976, he moved to Calgary and after two years to Vancouver, where he practiced law for almost 40 years, until retirement. He returned to Windsor in 2017, where he now resides with his wife Susan Vesala, and their cat, Sophie (*felis catis*).

The Brains (and Referee)

Susan Vesala is a native of Sault Ste. Marie, Ontario and was born in 1958. After high school she headed west to Edmonton, Alberta where she got a position at the Canadian Broadcasting Corporation as a technician. She later made it to the west coast and worked for CBC Vancouver for several years. In 1992 she moved to Belize, where she built and ran a successful Bed & Breakfast on Ambergris Caye. Upon returning to Vancouver, she earned a certificate from UBC/BCIT as a Network Administration Security Professional. She researched, formatted, and advised on many aspects of this book. She is married to the editor.

CPSIA information can be obtained
at www.ICGtesting.com
Printed in the USA
LVHW080231220421
685204LV00015B/986